177

(16)

RESEARCH HIGHLIGHTS 9

Social Work in Rural and Urban Areas

Department of Social Work
University of Aberdeen
King's College
Aberdeen

RESEARCH HIGHLIGHTS NUMBER NINE

Social Work in Rural and Urban Areas

Editor: Joyce Lishman
Secretary: Margaret Donald
Editorial Adviser: Professor G. Rochford
University of Aberdeen
Department of Social Work
King's College
Aberdeen
June 1984

Published by Department of Social Work
University of Aberdeen
King's College
Aberdeen

Manuscripts prepared by
Omega Information Services Limited
Aberdeen

ISBN 0 9505999 8 0

Printed by Skeneprint Limited
Broadfold Road
Bridge of Don Industrial Estate
Aberdeen AB2 8EE

LIST OF CONTENTS

CONTRIBUTORS

Joyce Lishman	Her Ph.D research at Aberdeen University analyses social workers' behaviour in interviews using videotapes and explores the relationship between this behaviour and prognosis and outcome. Previously a social worker in child and adolescent psychiatry. Publications include 'A Clash in Perspective? A Study of Worker and Client Perceptions of Social Work' British Journal of Social Work, 8, 3, 1974, a study of her own practice.
Greg Lloyd	Lecturer in Economics in the Department of Land Economy at the University of Aberdeen. He has a research background in the rural economy with a specific interest in land ownership.
Siobhan Lloyd	Lecturer in Social Policy and Community Work in the Department of Social Work, University of Aberdeen. Formerly a community worker in Speke, Liverpool and with Merseyside Council for Voluntary Service. Current research funded by SWSG evaluating the establishment of Designated Places under the Criminal Justice (Scotland) Act 1980.
Geoffrey Brogden	A former Principal Lecturer in Social Work, Suffolk College, now free-lance lecturer and welfare benefits advisor. Previous experience as a probation officer and social worker. Member of BASW Poverty Panel and editor of Benefit's page for British Unemployed Resource Network Newsletter.

Gordon Grant — Director of the Care Networks Project research team in the Department of Social Theory & Institutions, University College of North Wales, Bangor. Between 1977 and 1982 he and his colleagues were engaged in studies of service delivery systems and dependency groups in rural areas. This also involved major replication exercises with research teams in Birmingham, East Anglia and Kent. His present research involves an investigation into the dynamics of care for mentally handicapped adults and their families. This is part of a larger study which embraces the older elderly, elderly people suffering from dementia and their carers. He received his M.Sc. and Ph.D. at the University of Manchester Institute of Science and Technology.

Emilia Martinez-Brawley — Associate Professor of Social Welfare at the Pennsylvania State University. Publications include articles in the area of rural social work and rural social service delivery in the Journal of Education for Social Work, Arete, the Community Development Journal, Human Services in the Rural Environment, Sociology and Social Welfare, the NASW News. She has studied rural social work in the U.S. and has also carried out a number of international studies in Latin America, Great Britain and the Republic of Ireland, and is author of three books: Pioneer Efforts in Rural Social Welfare (Penn State Press, 1980), Seven Decades of Rural Social Work (Praeger, 1981) and Rural Social and Community Work in the U.S. and Britain. Dr. Martinez-Brawley is active in the National Rural Social Work Caucus, is a member of the national board of NASW, and of the Commission of Accreditation of CSWE.

Philip Seed	Senior Lecturer in the Department of Social Work, University of Aberdeen. Previous experience includes Family Service Units, Local Authority work with the elderly and handicapped, and residential experience with maladjusted children. Author of two recent books based on research : All Kinds of Care (with Margaret Thomson) published by Scottish Academic Press, and Mental Handicap: Who Helps in Rural and Remote Communities? published by Costello Educational, 1981.
Gillian Dalley	MRC Research Sociologist, MRC Medical Sociology Unit, Aberdeen, presently working on a study of the attitudes of professionals working in the health and social services towards current policies relating to the care of chronically dependent people. Previously worked for Women's Aid and in Welfare Rights. Recent publications include articles on nursing homes for the elderly (in Ageing in Modern Society, (ed) D. Jerrome) and the assumptions underlying current community care policies (in Critical Social Policy, 8, 1983).
Stuart Watts	Entered social work as a Community Service Volunteer in 1968, worked as a volunteer co-ordinator in South Wales until 1969 then as volunteer co-ordinator with Task Force in Islington until 1971. Employed by London Borough of Southwark as Community Worker in Peckham for one year then trained at Polytechnic of North London for 2 years qualified 1972. Worked for Aberdeenshire and Kincardine Social Work Department based at Stonehaven 3 years and then moved to Huntly in the Gordon Division of Grampian Region where he has worked for the past 9 years (7 of which as a single practitioner).

EDITORIAL

Joyce Lishman

'Social Work in Rural and Urban Areas' is a particularly appropriate title to be published in a 'boom' city set in the sparsely populated North of Scotland. In planning the volume three aims emerged:

1. to explore whether a rural/urban distinction is valid in general and what myths surround it;

2. to draw together the less than extensive relevant research and examine whether different implications for social service provision and practice arise according to setting, rural or urban;

3. to explore whether models developed as appropriate for one kind of area, urban or rural, could be applied to the other.

That the volume does not completely achieve these aims reflects in part four difficulties, inherent in the rural/urban discussion:

1. the definition of rural is problematic;

2. there are difficulties in data collection (see Brogden and Dalley, for example) including an urban bias, and the masking of local differences within averages for large areas.

3. research on the rural/urban dimension in the social services is, as the Lloyds and Seed point out, scarce;

4. research on the rural/urban distinction reflects different perspectives and assumptions and interpretation differs on that basis.

Many of the articles in this volume appear to reflect two distinct interpretations of the research evidence. Martinez-Brawley and Watts argue that a rural/urban distinction is valid and that a policy of centralisation, for example, has a particularly detrimental effect on rural areas. On the other hand Grant argues that the distinction is invalid and detracts from examination of other areas of central importance for social work, such as the relationship between formal and informal care.

There is a danger in taking a 'rural' perspective that problems may be attributed to rurality rather than social work in general. For example, themes of loss of individual autonomy and control of one's own work in social work are common and not confined to rural areas, but may appear, in the professional isolation of rural working, as particular phenomena of that setting.

There is a further danger of polarisation in the rural/urban discussion. Is any integration of the different perspectives possible? While some broad distinctions can be made about rural and urban populations in terms of area, distance, density of population, transport and resources, these contributions indicate that differences within a rural or urban area can be as great as those between them, and therefore attention should be paid to more specific localities and their differences, both in measurement of need and provision of services.

This does have implications for planning and service provision in that local needs may not be best identified and responded to by centralised planning authorities. A locality-specific approach and response implies diversity and local initiative and autonomy, which are not necessarily compatible with strong centralised control and decision making.

THE CHANGING CONTEXT OF RURAL SOCIAL WORK AND SERVICE DELIVERY

Greg Lloyd
and
Siobhan Lloyd

In 1980 the then Social Science Research Council published the findings of its major study of the inner city problem. The analysis was primarily concerned with the causes of concentrated economic decline, social deprivation and physical decay in the inner urban areas of British cities. One interesting part of the study was the report commissioned into the relevance of rural problems and its relationship to the mainstream inner city debate.

The rural study is in itself a fascinating contribution to our general understanding of rural problems and the social, economic and political processes at work in the British countryside. More importantly it reveals the attitudes and perceptions of researchers and policy makers to rural affairs. The approach and prescription tends to reflect the dominant urban ideology of both theoreticians and researchers and is relatively unsympathetic to the distinctive problems of the countryside.

The Social Science Research Council Report provides an ideal context for the ideas reflected in this particular issue of Research Highlights. It makes powerful observations about the current state of rural research in Britain when it argues that:

> 'the late 1970's witnessed an escalating concern for the socio-economic problems of rural Britain. Yet this had not found expression in analysis nor policy initiatives. The research that has been undertaken into rural areas has focussed on land use, conservation and recreational issues, depopulation and

"pressures on the countryside"'[1].

The quotation suggests two main features of contemporary rural research. In the first place it would appear that analysis of the countryside, in its widest sense, was until recently relatively neglected. Secondly, it would appear that there is a bias in existing research with an emphasis on the physical, land use and environmental problems of rural areas. In short there is a tendency for social and economic analysis to be under-represented with respect to the countryside. This emphasis is immediately recognisable in the recent controversial debate over the effects of modern agriculture on the environment. Research[2] has shown that the complex economics of farming in Britain have led to an increasing reliance on mechanisation, the increasing use of pesticides and other chemicals and the creation of larger farm units. These have had a marked effect, for example, on the landscape of lowland Britain, particularly by removing copses, hedgerows and walls. Perhaps the fact that relatively little is said about the resultant loss of labour in agriculture because of increasing use of machinery bears witness to the overriding concern with physical issues. The increasing number of environmental groups and lobbies in Britain also reflects this emphasis[3].

RURAL RESEARCH INITIATIVES

There is however a wealth of historical research findings relating to social and economic change and relationships in the countryside. The emergence of a capitalist economic order in Britain involved[4]:

> 'complex processes and procedures of institutional change, redistribution of economic and political power, and concerted, deliberate public policy efforts for redistributing the gains and losses inherent in economic growth'.

In the seventeenth, eighteenth and nineteenth centuries the contributions made by agriculture and rural areas to this process was a fundamental one. The conditions for the transition from feudalism to capitalism were facilitated by the prevailing form of land ownership, economic power and political control[5]. The period witnessed the emerging technological, economical and political pre-requisites for change[6]. It is commonly referred to as the 'agricultural revolution' or the 'age of improvement' the choice of term reflecting the historian's particular methodology and value judgements.

The effects of the broader economic and political transformations on the people living and working in the countryside were profound. In the first place there was the structural effect, such as the destruction of small scale peasant proprietors and the creation of landless agricultural wage labourers. Indeed it is suggested that the resultant

> 'trilogy of landlord, farmer and labourer characterised Victorian rural society and formed the basis of both contemporary and current images of the rural world'[7].

The conditions of different social groups are also well documented, for example, the farm labourers or servants, the gentry, the small tenant farmers and the established landed orders[8]. Furthermore historical research sheds considerable light on the effects of such fundamental changes in different parts of rural Britain. An excellent example is the crofting communities in the remote Highlands and Islands of Scotland[9]. Here the expropriation of land by the landlords, who were descended from the old clan chieftains; the enforced clearance of the population; the use of land for profit through sheep and deer, and the creation of crofting townships are a specific manifestation of the capitalist transformation of rural Britain.

In the light of this wealth of information it is perhaps surprising that the momentum of interest in social research and economic issues has not been maintained to the present. The reasons for this are complex, but some contributory factors could include the glorification of the rural way of life, the dominance of interest in urban problems and research, and the disjointed development of rural sociology in the earier post war period.

The glorification of rural life was created by urban dwellers in the nineteenth century. The imagery is a familiar one;

> 'conventional portrayals of the English village remain almost unashamedly bucolic, influenced in particular by the evocation of familiar sights and sounds - thatched cottages, village greens, lush meadows, the songs of birds, the ringing of church bells. Even work on the land is commonly supposed to be more morally beneficial, more metaphysically rewarding and hence less tainted by "mere" monetary considerations than any other form of employment'[10].

The belief in such a 'rural idyll' is the source of, and is itself supported by, a number of myths about rural life. A classic example is that the cost of living is much lower in the countryside. This is based on the premise that people living in the rural areas can grow their own food and hence be self sufficient. This myth has been recently exploded by the findings of a study into cost inflation in rural Scotland[11].

Complementing this sanguine attitude to rural social and economic conditions has been the dominance of urban issues within social research in Britain. Despite the fundamental changes that occurred in the British countryside during the agricultural and industrial revolutions, there appears to have been an overriding concern with the appalling conditions of the rapidly expanding industrial towns and cities. It is not necessary to quantify this bias in terms of citing the numerous publications on urban sanitary and housing conditions, the poverty of the factory work place, the exploitation of women and children, the actions of ruthless landlords and property speculators, the corruption of local authorities, the struggle for reform, standards and environmental controls and faltering attempts at municipal socialism. It would also be wrong to claim that these conditions were worse in rural areas; it suffices to note that by and large greater emphasis was given to the urban circumstances, and less attention paid as a consequence to the rural situation.

Finally there is the disjointedness and polarisation of sociological analyses of rural society and economy. In the post war period sociologists began increasingly to undertake studies of communities located in remoter rural areas[12]. This approach was primarily descriptive and anthropological in that the inhabitants of the remote communities were being observed for discernible 'rural' traits. Moreover, the studies were highly localised and therefore highly specific. This phase of rural sociological work has since been severely criticised[13], on the grounds that the methodology did not consider the prevailing and historical distribution of power in the rural societies, nor the social stratification in the countryside. More recent studies have attempted to redress this balance, and have examined the ideological, political and social dimension to change in rural Britain[14]. Caution must be exercised, however, as this wider sociological perspective is confined to a specific area of lowland Britain, viz East Anglia, with few studies carried out in other areas. Significant differences in circumstance do exist, and the dangers of basing rural policy on such narrow evidence for the remainder of rural Britain must be recognised[15].

THE RELEVANCE OF A RURAL DIMENSION?

A discussion of whether a rural dimension to social policy and social work delivery exists should correctly be preceded by a definition of 'rural'. This is of course a controversial area and has led to considerable debate as to the optimal criteria to adopt [16]. It also begs the question of whether a precise definition of rural is necessary, as there are considerable variations within rural areas. The Countryside Commission for example defines 98% of the Scottish land mass as 'countryside' - but this definition masks the differences between the remote west and north, and the extra-urban hinterland of the south and east.

Equally controversial, but for the purposes of this issue of Research Highlights, more applicable, is the question of whether there is a rural-urban dichotomy of social policy making and service delivery. There is no clear consensus on this issue, as the individual papers illustrate.

Seed, in discussing residential and day care facilities in rural areas, and Brogden, focussing on deprivation, both argue for a specific rural perspective to policy and service delivery. They stress the difficulties of assessing need in the countryside and the consequent inherent tendency to underprovision of services in rural areas. Similarly they argue that the 'costs' of service delivery are higher in rural areas. Costs in this respect may include tangible financial costs and the intangible considerations such as physical inaccessibility and inconvenience. Their view is supported by Watts, who writes of the experiences of social work practice in 'the sticks'. The conclusion to be drawn from their arguments is that the issue of 'locality' is of central importance: the fact that the problem, policy and implementation takes place in a rural settingsomehow makes it different. Because of this the difference must, on the grounds of 'ruralness', be compensated. It could be argued that such an argument tends to ignore the political realities of its logic. Could the rural areas command greater control over resources for such services on the basis of such arguments?

An alternative approach taken by Grant is to stress the 'structural' dimension to rural areas. Grant discusses in detail the question of the existence of a dichotomy between rural and urban areas in terms of social care, and argues that

> 'the key challenges facing those with an interest in developing social care are essentially the same in both rural and urban areas. The issues at stake have little to do with the supposed rural-urban dichotomy. They are part of wider debates about the balance between family, community and state intervention; the equation between consumer participation, choice or sovereignty and professional expertise; and the building of structures which promote participative democracy and which serve rather than service the community'.

Grant's central thesis is that the realities of life in town and country are not dissimilar, and he concludes that 'in the present system the rural/urban debate is dead'.

The debate between what may be termed the 'locational' and 'structural' explanations of rural problems is not new[17]. The literature on the existence of 'regional' and 'inner city' problems exhibits the same tension. The 'regional' economic problems of high unemployment, disinvestment, low productivity and a failure to diversify the industrial base in, for example, the central belt of Scotland or the north east of England may be attributed to the specific economic structure of the area and the high cost of its particular location. A more accurate explanation is perhaps to be derived from an amalgamation of the structural and locational explanations[18].

Within the rural context, this has been refined in terms of identifying the commonality between urban and rural deprivation, together with the distinguishing features of each. The end result is in effect a fusion of structural and locational factors which give the countryside its specific problems. This is outlined in Table 1.

In the light of these considerations it is difficult to criticise the observation, that

> 'the same basic conditions of industrial decline, unemployment, poverty, housing and social distress that are to be found in urban communities also exist in the rural areas (of England and Wales) in varying degrees of extent and severity. However because these conditions are to be found in small pockets dispersed over rural areas as a whole, they are not so readily identifiable as in the case of the inner city, and tend to be ignored'[19].

The argument that, rural deprivation exists, may be restated as follows. Firstly, there is an imbalance in the distribution of opportunities between rural areas and elsewhere (the structural factor); secondly, within the rural areas the inequalities resulting from this imbalance are magnified by the interaction of a range of economic, physical, cultural and political factors (the locational perspective); finally, the result is a situation in which the problems of disadvantaged individuals and groups are exacerbated and the problem increases[20].

The latter effect is a consequence of a number of factors, including a failure to recognise the complexities of economic and social relationships in rural areas. There are a number of facets to this neglect.

Firstly, it is forgotten by policy makers concerned with the countryside that employment and housing issues are often interlinked. This is a common feature on farms, estates or in larger scale non-farm based employment. In Speyside, for example, one of

Table 1

Problems in Urban and Rural Britain

INNER URBAN

Physical environment	**Economic stagnation**	**Inaccessibility**
derelict land	Declining demand for labour	to services and jobs
blighted land	high unemployment	
visual/noise pollution	low wages	**High per-capita costs** of services (public and private)
	wrong skills	
Racial tension	poor job opps. for school-leavers	**High % of elderly people**
Overt delinquency		
	Population decline loss of dynamic element	effects on society
Problems from over-crowding		costs of servicing
	Decline in services (public and private)	
lack of open space		
stress of high-rise life	**Little new investment** (public or private)	
	Gentrification/ second homes	
	Declining morale and community spirit	
	Housing markets which 'lock in' the poor	

Source: Moseley, [18].

OUTER RURAL

the local distilleries is faced with closure. Not only will substantial redundancies ensue, but also a large number of people will be made homeless as tied housing is lost. Since rural public authorities have neither a large public sector stock nor building programme to compensate for such a loss of housing the problem of homelessness can be seen as a hidden facet to rural life.

This complexity is also illustrated by recent trends in population and migration. There has been a marked urban-rural shift[21], which itself has endorsed the physical changes in those areas of countryside lying adjacent to the major conurbations[22]. At the same time rural depopulation continues, largely as a result of declining employment opportunities in the remoter areas. The structural effects of this transfer must not be ignored by policy makers, yet at present little recognition of its complexity is evident[23].

Secondly, there is the problem of data, and particularly its availability and applicability to the problems of rural areas. This is an issue to which the contributors of the papers in Research Highlights return time and again. Brogden clearly shows how the conventional indices, which are applicable to urban areas, present a distorted view of the countryside. Deprivation indices suggest that the greatest concentrations are to be found in urban areas. Grant goes further by arguing that the incompatibility constrains viable comparison between urban and rural conditions. However, there appears to remain a wish to construct indices which do enable a rural-urban comparison. A recent study argued;

> 'it was agreed that the definition of deprivation should be applicable in both rural and urban settings though clearly the cause of deprivation may be different, for example, people might be deprived of supportive relationships in either setting but in a rural area the cause might be geographical isolation whereas in a town it might be overcrowding, making people compete with and be threatened by each other'[24].

The complexity of the data problem is further explored by Dalley, in relation to health care. She suggests that the aggregation of such data is confined to the regional level and little attention is paid to intra-regional comparisons. This level of data masks considerable variations between urban and rural areas, but also between different degrees of remoteness in the countryside. This latter point is raised by Martinez-Brawley who discusses the controversial economic debate concerning core-periphery relationships. This suggests that remote areas are under-developed in an economic, social and material sense. In short they have been overlooked by the prevailing economic order. A glance however at the economic history of the Highlands and Islands of Scotland, for example, reveals that their present day problems are a consequence of past market forces, and not the result of the failure of such forces penetrating the Highland economy[25].

Thirdly, there is the issue of access to information, also noted by contributors to this volume. It is often argued that because of the rural characteristics of a relatively dispersed population, and the recognised ethic of self help and reliance, people in rural areas do not demand or need the level of services provided in urban areas. Dalley notes this in relation to health care provision. Research however indicates that the low level of demand is more a function of poor information about the availability of services than satisfaction with existing ones. The Cleator Moor Community Development Project[26] demonstrated there was no less need for information services in a rural setting than in an urban environment. Furthermore although informal networks of care did exist in the countryside, they were incapable of coping with the range of problems and inquiries presented in a satisfactory way. Watts would probably share this view from a practitioner's stance. The implications of this are far-reaching. On the one hand:

> 'traditional roles have to change; the social worker for example could not hope to deliver a person to person casework service over a large area. More work might have to be done through other people, becoming a kind of supervisor/consultant to the vicar, the neighbour or the parish clerk. Interdisciplinary boundaries would have to become more blurred with, for instance, doctor, health visitor and social worker coming close to interchangeability'[27].

Alternatively, as Martinez-Brawley and Watts point out, social workers must look beyond the tenets of specialisation and casework if they are to provide a meaningful service to dispersed populations. The extent to which this approach can be put into practice has already been identified as an important issue[28]. However experience from the Cumbrian example shows that where an information centre was established in a rural area, families who would traditionally have been expected to refer themselves to the statutory-welfare services, approached the centre with issues which it could not provide given its remit. The conclusion therefore in this case was for the demystification of statutory procedures and a wider remit for social workers.

This debate is largely the result of designing social policies for rural areas with assumptions better suited to the physical and political circumstances of urban areas. The ability of the population to participate in local decision making is important, particularly in the complex procedures of the town and country planning system. One example is that of Grampian Regional Council's attempt to involve the rural public in its Rural Area Structure Plan. Because of its earlier experiences, it decided to involve the public through the innovatory mechanism of the rural community councils and associations. The effectiveness of this approach and the lessons learnt from it are discussed elsewhere[29]. What is revealing about the exercise is that the Regional Council implicitly assumed the rural public had the opportunities to acquaint themselves with the proposals in the Structure Plan. The difficulties of this in a dispersed population encompassing remote areas, and at a time of high winter, appears to have been overlooked by the planners and politicians.

A further result of this exercise is presented in Table 2. This shows that the problem is not completely dictated by locational factors. The real problem lies with the general ignorance by the public of structure planning. This is in part a result of the failure of planning authorities to demystify planning and promote involvement and participation by the public.

Finally, there are the political complexities of the countryside. Research indicates that in many rural areas the prevailing ideology is that of self reliance and independence. This is of course fostered by the distribution of power in rural areas, which reflects the conservative ideology of rural ruling classes[30]. A further problem is the lack of real interest and understanding by the political parties. The dominance of the conservative ideology in the countryside is no excuse for the ignorance prevailing elsewhere [31]. It is best summed up in the following quotation,

> 'the three per cent of the population who work in agriculture sit in their laager, alternatively romanticised and despised by the rest of us, producing goods whose value makes agriculture the most important industry in the country. And yet so completely is agriculture ignored by the Labour Party that any ambitious MP who can distinguish a cow from a sheep has an excellent chance of becoming Labour's agricultural spokesman'[32].

However the four issues do not represent the full complexity of the rural question today. We now turn to examine how the papers in this volume contribute to our knowledge and understanding.

AN OVERVIEW

As a collection these papers demonstrate the lack of agreement and current confusion with many of the issues referred to elsewhere in this paper. A brief resume of some of their main points may serve to illustrate.

Dalley concentrates her argument on the location-allocation debate. These two features point to the significance of locality in the delivery of services, yet it is pointed out that most comparative studies stop short of examining intra-regional trends, which would better demonstrate the existence or not of rural differences in the provision of health care. A further gap is that the differences between the rural areas themselves have not been comprehensively investigated and identified. It is argued that small scale qualitative studies are largely seen in isolation and may therefore show no demonstrable disadvantage in rural areas as a whole or between one rural area and another. Larger scale studies, on the other hand may only confirm the disadvantages of rural areas in relation to urban areas, rather than in relation to each other. Dalley also makes a case for the incorporation of consumer feedback on services but acknowledges that, depending on the client group studied, a positive result may have more to do with acceptability of what already exists than with the existence of a better quality of service.

Table 2

Reasons given by community councils why consultations with the public about structure plans produce little response

Structure plans have little relevance	8%
The relevance of structure plans is not obvious	35%
Structure plans are hard to understand	35%
Efforts to consult the public are inadequate	22%
People are unaware of structure plans	30%
Other	43%

NB Not mutually exclusive

Source: Lloyd, G., Reid, C. Rowan Robinson, J. Shucksmith, M. (1980) (29).

The issue of locality is also central to Grant's argument but he makes the strongest plea for rejecting the urban/rural dichotomy. His main premise is that other issues (for example, the relationship between formal and informal caring networks and the need to examine the way in which caring networks are instigated in both urban and rural settings) take precedence. An extension of this argument is that the challenges to social service delivery in both areas are similar.

The importance of locality therfore is seen to lie in the ability of both statutory and non-statutory agencies to reflect and serve local need, and to organise services accordingly. Grant's paper however fails to place the argument or evidence within any political or economic context. He does however give a different perspective to Dalley's reference to consumer satisfaction by suggesting that 'community norms' may have an important part to play in the way in which services are used.

Brogden, who, interestingly concentrates a substantial part of his argument on evidence from urban studies, suggests compiling a different set of indices with which to measure rural deprivation. However he too acknowledges the limitations imposed by available data and suggests that lower morbidity rates in rural areas are masking unmet needs rather than a function of satisfaction with existing services. He also adheres to the view that spatial differences do exist between urban and rural areas.

Seed too suggests giving more attention to debates on locality but firmly concludes that rural/urban differences form an essential backdrop to our understanding of the needs of individual localities. In this way he argues, services can become responsive to local areas and the tension between planning and operational components of social service provision is partly reduced.

Turning to social work practice, both Martinez-Brawley and Watts return to well worn arguments centering on specialism versus genericism and patch versus non patch based social work. Martinez-Brawley seems in some doubt with her conclusions, and argues that generalism and genericism may both be appropriate, but that in Britain at least the debate about genericism versus specialism remains unresolved. Watt suggests, perhaps cynically, that rural social workers rather than rationally deciding their preferred modus operandi for rural areas, are forced to work as generalists due to a lack of resources. Both authors also raise the issue of whether casework oriented social work or community work are more appropriate forms of activity for rural areas. However Watts unpacks this further by suggesting that the difference in social work tasks in rural areas, rather than any difference in the range of problems confronting such areas, demands a different response from social work.

A TENTATIVE CONCLUSION

The issues raised in these papers are concerned with a relatively neglected aspect of the welfare state of Britain and come at an interesting time. Just as there is an upsurge of interest in the countryside, and a recognition that people living and working in rural areas do suffer from the problems experienced in towns and cities, so the pendulum swings against government involvement.

The ideology of the market has gained a substantial hold in Britain. The present government is committed to restructuring the role of the state in relation to welfare. The level and orientation of government spending and control is being changed and the liberalisation of the economy is well under way. In political terms rural society is not exempt from this trend with the balance of power increasingly located centrally. The social values of this tendency are claimed to be Victorian. If that is so, then social relationships in the countryside will very rapidly come full circle. The outlook for rural social work is not optimistic, and there is an urgent need for a radical reappraisal of its role by both practitioners and policy makers.

References

1. Moseley, M. 'The Relevance of Rural Development to the Inner City Debate' Social Science Research Council, 9, London, 1980.
2. Shoard, M. The Theft of the Countryside. Maurice Temple Smith, 1980.
   Norton Taylor, R. Whose Land is it Anyway? Agriculture, Planning and Land Use in the British Countryside. Turnstone Press Ltd., 1982.
3. Lowe, P. & Goyder, J. Environmental Groups in Politics. Allen & Unwin, 1983.
4. Dorner, P. Land Reform and Economic Development. Penguin, Harmondsworth, 1972.

5. Massey, D. & Catalano, A. Capital and Land. Landownership by Capital in Great Britain. Edward Arnold, 1978.
6. Butlin, R.A. The Transformation of Rural England c.1580-1800. Oxford University Press, 1982.
7. Scott, J. The Upper Classes. Property and Privilege in Britain. Macmillan, 1980.
8. Mingay, G.E. Rural Life in Victorian England. Futura Books, 1979.
Horn, P. Labouring Life in the Victorian Countryside. Gill and Macmillan, 1976.
Horn, P. The Rural World 1780-1850. Social Change in the English Countryside. Hutchinson, 1980.
9. Hunter, J. The Making of the Crofting Community. John Donald, 1976.
10. Newby, H. Green and Pleasant Land. Social Change in Rural England. Penguin, Harmondsworth, 1979.
11. Scottish Consumer Council. Consumer Problems in Rural Areas. Glasgow, 1982.
12. Kallberg, S. Report from a Swedish Village. Pelican, 1969.
Aalen, F. & Brody, H. Gola: Life and Last Days of an Island Community. Mercier, Cork, 1969.
Franklin, S. Rural Societies. PaperMac, 1971.
Blythe, R. Akenfield: Portrait of an English Village. Penguin, Harmodsworth, 1972.
Brody, H. Inishkillane: Change and Decline in the West of Ireland. Pelican, 1973.
13. Benvenuti, B., Galjart, B. & Newby, H. 'The Current Status of Rural Sociology' Sociologica Ruralis. 15(1/2), 1975, 3-21.
Newby, H. 'Rural Sociology' Current Sociology. 28(1) 1980, 1-109.
14. Newby, H. The Deferential Worker. Penguin, Harmondsworth, 1977.
15. Newby, H., Bell, C., Rose. D, & Saunders, P. Property, Paternalism and Power. Class and Control in Rural England. Hutchinson, 1978.
16. Shucksmith, D.M. & Lloyd, G. 'Rural Planning in Scotland: a critique' Countryside Planning Yearbook. 4, 1983, 103-128.
17. Cloke, P.J. 'An Index of Rurality for England and Wales'. Regional Studies. 11, 1977, 31-46.
Scottish Development Department. Rural Indicators Research. Scottish Office, January, 1978.
Cullingford, D. & Openshaw, S. 'Identifying Areas of Rural

Deprivation Using Social Area Analysis' Regional Studies. 16(6), 1982, 409-418.

18. Stilwell, F. Regional Economic Policy. Papermac, 1972.
Moseley, M. 'Is Rural Deprivation Really Rural?' The Planner. 66(4), 1980, 97-98.

19. Association of District Councils. Rural Recovery: Strategy For Survival. London, 1978.

20. McLaughlin, B.P. 'Rural Deprivation' The Planner. 67(2), 1981, 31-33.

21. Forsythe, D. Planning Implications of Urban-Rural Migration. Gloucester College of Arts and Technology, October, 1983.

22. Cheshire, P. 'Onslaught on the Countryside - or how Field Copse Vanished!' New Society. 22 September 1983, 428-430.

23. Shaw, J.M. 'Rural Planning in 1980: An Overview' The Planner. 66. 1980. 88-90.

24. Herts & Worcestershire County Council. Rural Community Development Project: Report of the Working Party October 1975-June 1978. RCDP, 1978.

25. Carter, I. 'The Highlands of Scotland as an Underdeveloped Region' in de Kadt, E. & Williams, G. (Eds.) Sociology and Development. Tavistock, London, 1974. 279-311.

26. Butcher, M., Cole, I. & Glen, A. Information and Action Services for Rural Areas - a case study in Cumbria. Dept. of Social Administration and Social Work, University of York, 1975.

27. Stroud, J. 'Social Welfare Delivery in Rural Areas' Social Work Service. No. 23, June 1980.

28. Williams, G. Rural Self Help - Institutional Instrument or Policy Objective in Rural Development? Paper presented to 8th International Seminar on Marginal Regions, Wales, August 1983.

29. Lloyd, G., Reid, C., Rowan Robinson, J. & Shucksmith, M. Grampian Rural Area Structure Plan: The Community Council Response. University of Aberdeen, Community Councils and Public Participation Working Paper, 2, May 1984.

30. Rose, D., Saunders, P., Newby, H. & Bell, C. 'Ideologies of Property: A Case Study' Sociological Review, 24(4), 1976, 699-730.

31. The Labour Party. Out of Town. Out of Mind. A Programme for Rural Revival. The Labour Party, 1981.

32. Carter, I. 'Rural Rides' (A Book Review) New Statesman, 2 November 1979, 685-686.

DEPRIVATION IN URBAN AND RURAL AREAS: NEEDS, IDENTIFICATION AND POLICY

Geoffrey Brogden

INTRODUCTION

During the 1960's and 1970's researchers and politicians became increasingly aware of spatial concentrations of deprivation. The inner city areas of old, deteriorating housing had always been recognised physically as such areas. Yet when measures of deprivation other than poor housing (such as low pay, unemployment or sickness of breadwinner, large families and single parent families) were used, it became obvious that outer urban areas, particularly areas of council housing, shared with the inner areas some features of spatially concentrated deprivation. For a time identification of such areas and positive discrimination in allocating resources to such areas seemed to offer an attractive political solution to the persistence of poverty and deprivation. The Educational Priority Areas, the Community Development Projects and their successors were founded on this concept of spatial concentration of deprivation[1][2][3].

Post-war planning policy, which saw the major conurbations as overcrowded, and sought to decant substantial proportions of their populations to New Towns or expanded overspill areas, tended to increase concentrations of deprivation in the inner city, as the younger, better educated and more skilled workers and their families moved out, leaving behind the elderly, the unskilled, the low-paid and recent immigrants. Employers faced with cramped sites in the old cities, planning restrictions, and a largely unskilled labour force, also moved to the green field sites.

This process was accentuated by changing practice in shipping and transporting goods, particularly the coming of the container[4][5]. The results are only too evident in the empty acres of the once proud London and Liverpool docklands, and elsewhere.

Planners and local authorities faced with a disparity between local resources based on the (comparatively) deteriorating property values, and local needs of a population which by its very structure placed a greater than average demand on services, lobbied for a greater share of central government 'equalisation' money. Thus Eversley[6] in a seminal article in 1972 compared the falling population of Greater London and the rate burden on that population with the increasing population and lower per capita rate burden of the populations of the six South Eastern counties surrounding London. Eversley sought to show that, not only in London, but in the largest county boroughs outside London, population was falling, the rate of increase in total rateable value was less than the average for England and Wales and, with constant costs, the rate burden per capita was greater than average. Similarly gross loan debt per head was shown to be increasing faster in the cities than in other parts of England and Wales, and to be significantly higher than average in the largest county boroughs. Whilst Eversley sought to show that needs were greater in the old urban areas because of differential migration, he made no attempt to assess the quality of services in the 'low rate' areas, other than in terms of the quality of social capital, mainly in relation to the built environment.

Rural areas at a greater distance from the large cities were also experiencing problems of declining population, job loss and worn-out social capital. Attempts to use the Census to develop indicators of social malaise, and spatial concentrations of deprivation were bound to produce an urban bias. Census indicators showing proximity of households with high scores on indices of unemployment, large families, New Commonwealth origin, low educational achievement and poor housing conditions were seized upon as being (in combination) identifying attributes of areas of deprivation. The available non-urban indicators such as low density of population, high concentration of agricultural employment, and methods of transport used to get to work were not examined until the County and District Councils began to draw attention to their implications at the end of the 1970's.

Thus Holterman's work[7][8], attempting to sift out individual enumeration districts that produced high concentrations of deprivation on Census indicators, started from the assumption that such concentrations were not to be found in the local government designated Rural Districts. Whilst I and other commentators would argue that it is necessary to develop a different set of indices with which to measure rural deprivation, it seems unfortunate that the indices found significant in the urban context were not checked against a small sample of rural enumeration districts. Certainly my own very small scale research[9] suggests that on housing condition indices at least, some rural enumeration districts would have been well within Holterman's 'worst 5 per cent' measure.

Townsend's massive 1968 study of poverty in the United Kingdom[3] did not make any prior assumptions about urban concentration. He found that the percentage of the population in rural areas that was poor or marginally poor was not markedly different from that in urban or conurban areas. The lack of uniformity in data from rural areas is commented upon by Townsend, who also shows that nearly a third of the rural population, compared with a quarter elsewhere, lived in areas where over 50 per cent of the population had low incomes. Yet paradoxically a larger proportion than elsewhere were found to be living in high income areas.

From the discussion so far it is possible to detect four major trends in the attempts to measure spatial concentrations of deprivation. These are the concept of needs - for adequate housing, employment, education and social services; the concept of resources available within an area to meet identified need; the concept of life-style or 'standard of living' and the concept of quality of services available to meet need. In the following discussion the overlapping nature of these four concepts will become apparent.

One limitation on the researcher is the spatial areas for which data is available. Much material is only available on a regional or at best a local authority basis. Measurements based on such large areas have severe limitations in their usefulness for identifying deprived areas.

A statistical average or mean for such large areas inevitably hides considerable disparities within those areas, and the effect of this,

I will argue, has been to hide pockets of relatively severe deprivation within areas that show above average scores on usual indices. With the advent of speedy and cheap analysis of data by microcomputer it is becoming theoretically possible to develop indices by which such pockets of deprivation could be identified. The question will remain as to whether in an era of stable or declining resources such measures have any useful practical purpose.

In what follows I will attempt to evaluate some of the studies of area deprivation in the fields of employment, housing, health and social services, and information and advice.

EMPLOYMENT

Clearly people are deprived if they do not have access to job opportunities. The CDP studies clearly identified job loss in most of the Inner City areas in which they were established[10][11][12]. Thus the Canning Town CDP revealed the loss of 17,800 industrial jobs between 1966 and 1972 within its area[4]. Newham Borough, a typical pocket of deprivation within an otherwise prosperous and non-deprived region, did not have assisted area status, although subsequently part of the area (including Silvertown) has become the responsibility of the Dockland Development Commission. Despite these job losses between 1966 and 1972, government incentives were still available instead for firms considering moving to the Development and Assisted Areas and the New and Expanded towns.

Within rural areas similar inconsistencies occur. On regional counts both East Anglia and the South West have comparatively low unemployment rates and although 'Assisted Area' status was given to some parts of the South West region, no such designation was afforded the coastal resorts of East Anglia. Some surprising place names appear when winter unemployment rates for individual employment exchange areas are compared with regional rates. Thus in December 1983 Ilfracombe (28.4) and Hunstanton (28.1) were the areas with the highest percentage unemployment in England, and were surpassed only by Northern Ireland areas, and Tenby in Wales throughout the rest of the United Kingdom[13].

Thus it can be seen that there is inconsistency in officially recognising areas of high unemployment and allocating central government assistance, even given a scheme that seeks to identify small areas within regions that constitute pockets of deprivation.

Whilst the decline in employment in the traditional (and mainly urban) heavy industries has attracted much attention, the parallel post-war and continuing decline in employment in agriculture has excited little interest. Yet as the National Council for Voluntary Organisations shows[14] the full-time agricultural work-force declined at a rate of 4 per cent per annum in the 1960's, 2 per cent in the 1970's, and is back at the 4 per cent rate in the arable areas at least in the early 1980's.

Table 1

Regular Full Time Workers In Agriculture - County of Suffolk

1977	1978	1979	1980	1981	1982
5761	5605	5447	5227	4959	4833

Source:- Ministry of Agriculture - Census of Agricultural work-force[15].

Allied to this decline of the traditional rural employment base NCVO show a net loss of population of young people in many rural areas. This net loss is arrived at by comparing the 1961 Census 5-14 age group with the 1971 Census 15-24 age group in rural areas. The rural areas of Wales, the South West, Northern and Eastern England show such a loss. It is interesting that using county-wide figures Suffolk shows a net increase of young people on this measurement, whereas my own studies showed for two rural areas within Suffolk a net loss of between 16 and 25 per cent males and 23 to 25 per cent females[9].

Female economic activity rates are another important indicator of deprivation, particularly when they can be linked spatially with indicators of pay-levels. Areas with high job-loss, high registered unemployment, and high migration of young people are frequently also areas of low pay[3].

When such areas also have a low level of female economic activity, then there is likely to be a high incidence of low per capita income and a reliance on state benefits for a significant proportion of total family income. Thomas and Winyard[16] and Packman[17] show the clear links between these factors in rural areas. Not only are female economic activity rates low in rural areas, but the lack of opportunities combined with the incidence of seasonal work, leads to considerable under-employment. The East Anglian Regional Strategy team[18] has developed a useful measure of deviation from the regional average for access to employment opportunities, using a graded 'contour' map projection. Such a measure can be useful in determining the impact of employment policies through time, and has greater potential in identifying sub-regional pockets of employment deprivation. Holterman's[7] analysis of 1971 Census data shows that even restricting herself to the urban areas of the two most rural regions in England (East Anglia and the South West), produces a high percentage of enumeration districts in the worst 5 per cent range for low economic activity, both in males 15-49, and in females. The Association of County Council's analysis of rural areas on the female economic activity indicator confirms the low level for the rural employment areas within these regions[19].

The opportunities provided by local government reform in 1974, to take steps to discriminate positively in rural counties and districts by establishing the headquarter offices of the new councils in areas of restricted white collar employment, have in most cases been missed. In one East Anglian case the new district council rejected a small town for its headquarters on the grounds that the educational, shopping and recreational opportunities that it provided were too poor to attract local government officers. There was no sign that this had been weighed in the balance of possible improvement of these facilities with the advent of some hundreds of Social Class II & III staff in an area of marked migration of school-leavers[9]. In this particular case the rural town has lost facilities in the intervening years and retains its status as a pocket of deprivation in a county boasting a high expansion of both population and jobs.

HOUSING

Poor quality of housing as measured through lack of amenities, sharing of facilities, overcrowding and age of construction, has been consistently used as an indicator of urban deprivation. Although most post-war studies showed housing deprivation to be concentrated in the privately rented sector, by 1968, Townsend found that 'a larger proportion of the total population in structurally defective housing were in council housing than in all other rented property'[3]. Holterman's analysis[7] of the 1971 Census data found a concentration of enumeration districts which appeared in the worst 15 per cent on indices of overcrowding, lack of exclusive use of basic amenities, and male unemployment. In 43 local authorities there were 10 or more: 18.9 per cent of the total local authority population in Glasgow live in these enumeration districts and in England, Islington, Bradford, Salford and Kensington & Chelsea have the highest concentration.

However, as has already been shown, Holterman had deliberately excluded rural enumeration districts from her analysis. Yet the existence of rural areas with pockets of housing deprivation is shown in the 1971 Census: 20 per cent of households in Hartismere Rural District had <u>no</u> flush toilet[9], with similar figures applicable in many other rural districts.

Access to reasonable quality housing for the deprived is largely a matter of obtaining the tenure of local authority or voluntary sector housing. Average time spent on the waiting list before receiving an offer of a vacancy is a crucial measure of comparative deprivation and as might be expected the slow-down in local authority building and rehabilitation in recent years has led to a lengthening of this waiting time, and thus an increase in the number of families on the list. Harrison[20], in his work on Hackney, shows that the number of lettings available halved between 1977-8 and 1981-2 from 3,000 to 1,500. Thus in Hackney in 1977 the average wait for non-priority cases was three to four years but in 1979 had increased to eleven years.

Although it is to be expected that similar trends will be found in inner city areas there is less realisation of the crisis in local authority housing experienced in many rural areas. As Clark[21] shows local authority house-building rates have been low in rural areas, where less than 22 per cent of housing was owned by local authorities compared with the national average of 29 per cent in 1981. Between 1974 and 1979 half the houses built in England were constructed by local authorities or housing associations, but only 24 per cent in rural areas. It is more expensive to provide three or four units of housing in villages than it is for district councils to provide small estates in the larger villages or small towns within their area. This accelerates the tendency for the population base in villages to reduce relative to the operative level for provision of services such as schools, shops and transport, which in turn adds impetus to the decline of those small villages into dormitory, commuting or second home settlements[22].

Clark maintains that the take-up of the 'right to buy' provision in the Housing Act has been greater in rural areas at 8 per cent of the stock as opposed to 5 per cent national average. The 'rural safeguards' in the 1980 Act provide for re-purchase by local authorities in those areas designated by the Minister, but there is concern about the limited areas which have been designated[21][23]. In East Hampshire demand to buy council houses by sitting tenants has been much higher in the smaller villages which as Clark points out are the very places where planning policies limit new developments.

Sale of council houses in such villages means an overall reduction in houses for locals to rent in view of the virtual disappearance of long-term private rented property from these areas and the growth of 'holiday lets' and second homes. In South Hams in Devon, Phillips and Williams[24] found that potential housing choice for those who could not buy, and did not occupy 'tied' housing was very limited. In 1980 the waiting list stood at over 1,000 with only 120 to 150 lettings available per year to reduce it.

The possibility of 'reverse commuting' arises with families accepting housing in local towns rather than the village in which the head of the household works. If council houses bought in the small villages eventually become second or retirement homes, there are serious implications for the age structure and pattern of services for these settlements. Evidence also exists in rural areas of 'hidden need' which only comes to the surface if open surveys are carried out, for example leading in Allerdale District in Cumbria to the construction of council housing in a settlement in which no such housing previously existed. Of course no-one had their name down for a council house in the village as none existed, and it was only the survey that revealed the need[25].

Rural house prices are pushed up by those seeking retirement or holiday homes, and in rural areas when national house prices rise the increase may be disproportionate to the rise in incomes in traditional rural low-pay areas. The East Anglia Regional Strategy team show mortgage borrowers with markedly higher incomes than the regional average, and a steep rise in the deposit which it would be necessary to find to buy the average three bedroom house in East Anglia between 1966 and 1971 - from £651 to £1021 for a new house [18]. This reflects external influences on the house-purchase market and it is also the experience in the South-West region, and in holiday areas of Scotland[26]. Evidence of the characteristics of second-home buyers needs further study. It is the proportion of second homes in the village community that will be of paramount importance, combined with such factors as the proportion of 'outside' retiring households. Coleman[27] and Coles[28] provide useful models for work in this field.

Different factors affect the allocation of vacant council houses in urban and rural areas. Priority in urban areas often has to be given to those who are about to have their homes demolished for road, housing or other development, and next come the homeless and those with medical reasons for re-housing. In the rural areas local authorities are obliged to give priority to the occupiers of tied cottages where the farmer needs the cottage for another worker. The Rent (Agriculture) Act, 1976, provides for an advisory committee to assess the actual agricultural need for a house to be available to the farmer, and the urgency of that need. Official figures show applications by farmers under the Act in England running at approximately 560 per year from 1980-2 and 87 per cent of these cases were found to constitute an agricultural need, and therefore assumed a priority on local authority vacancies[29].

Clark[21] notes that the number of homelessness cases in rural areas has been growing in recent years particularly in those areas with an armed forces presence. The combination of these housing priority needs and a historically low base stock, with a high sales rate will need careful monitoring, together with an objective average income/house price index for these areas in order to assess how far rural workers are deprived in the local housing markets.

HEALTH AND SOCIAL SERVICES
(See also Dalley in this volume)

Higher than average mortality rates are statistically co-related with areas of urban deprivation, so that it is the areas of housing deprivation and heavy concentration of the economically inactive, and people in the lower socio-economic groups that have high rates of infant mortality[3][7]. Yet the OPCS and other statistics do not produce data for small areas such as census enumeration districts. The primary health care teams seem likely to be able to identify not only the highest risk families, but also the highest risk areas, and there is encouraging material on innovations in preventive care in a recent CPAG/NEC pamphlet[30].

The Black Report on Inequalities in Health was critical of the Resource Allocation Working Party criteria for re-distributing NHS resources. Black said that RAWP sought to bring about a more equitable distribution of resources between regions and within districts, 'without parallel attention as to how these resources are to be used'[31]. Black maintains that it is not sufficient to bring regions nearer the current average levels of expenditure in hospital and community health services, but it is necessary to review these resource allocations in the light of measured need. Black makes the case for a pronounced shift of resources to community and preventive health care, and argues for a programme of positive discrimination for ten special (urban) areas, those with the highest death rates when standardised for age and sex structure. Noting considerable differences in mortality rates within these ten areas, Black suggests development of criteria of health need related to smaller areas such as enumeration districts or wards.

Caution must be exercised in allowing low morbidity rates to influence resource allocation in rural areas, for not only have some of the rural regions had a low base of NHS resources, but there is room for some objective appraisal of low reported illness and contact with a doctor. Heller[32] shows that East Anglia had in 1974 resources per head of population that were 27.2 per cent below the national average for hospital services and 56.4 per cent below the national average for community health services. More data is needed as to whether low reported morbidity[33] is indicative of good health or of low contact with health services due to difficulties of access and/or a low level of available service affecting referral through low expectations. The age structure of some rural areas in which the elderly represent a higher than average proportion of the population suggests that statistically low morbidity rates may reflect considerable unmet need.

Rutter and Madge[34] review work on the geographical incidence of mental disorder, and confirm the much higher incidence in inner city areas than in rural counties. The detailed mapping of the Psychiatric Rehabilitation Association studies[35] of London and Sheffield show the correlation between the incidence of conditions resulting in referral to mental health services and the standard urban indices of deprivation, class, housing etc. Both Rutter and Madge and the PRA suggest some correlation of mental disorder with high population turn-over - not a feature usually associated with rural areas. Rutter and Madge note the persistence over time of high suicide and psychiatric disorder rates in particular areas and suggest that more research is needed to establish the reasons for these continuities.

Much of the work of personal social services does not lend itself to objective measurement that would tell us anything meaningful about comparative urban or rural deprivation. 'Expressed need' as measured by referral or continuing case-load rates is of limited value, when referral may be affected by anticipated availability or non-availability. As Shaw and Stockford[36] point out the concentration of Meals on Wheels and other domicillary services in the towns and larger villages may have influenced referral rates in rural areas. Although able to show considerably (76 per cent) lower provision of Meals on Wheels, and (20 per cent) lower provision of home helps per 1,000 population over 65, Shaw and Stockford can only point to the probability of greater hostility and stigmatisation of welfare recipients in rural areas, combined with low accessibility and lack of knowledge and information as factors influencing low expressed need.

Moseley[37] shows that in rural areas it is the elderly, children and teenagers, and housewives who suffer mobility deprivation, and it was the households without a car in rural Norfolk that were also likely to be without a phone, although about 90 per cent had a phone available to them within five minutes walk. The overlapping catchment areas of different services, the geographical re-organisations which reached epidemic proportions in post Seebohm Social Service Departments, and the 'trunk-call' distances often involved[9] combine to make self-referral by phone a frustrating and often expensive task in rural areas, where the option of a short bus ride to the office is not available.

As in urban areas it is the elderly who are likely to occupy pre-1919 houses (if not pre-1719 in rural areas) which by their structure and design increase daily living problems for their occupants. Yet the recent study of Day Centre provision for the elderly in Norfolk & Cambridgeshire shows that the number of places is significantly concentrated in the urban areas of these predominantly rural counties[3][8]. Thus while Day Centre places per 1,000 elderly per week were 17.83 in Norwich they only reached 4.33 in the rest of Norfolk: in Cambridge there were 47.0 Luncheon CLub places per 1,000 elderly per week, whilst only 14.53 places per 1,000 were available in rural Cambridgeshire. Stockford[39] revealed that one in six elderly people in Norfolk did not (1974) have access to a meals on wheels service and all of these old people lived in rural areas.

ADVICE AND INFORMATION

Access to information and advice has been described as the 'Fourth Right of Citizenship' in a National Consumer Council discussion paper[40]. They say 'Information ... is vital because the Welfare State has become even more complex, some would say labyrinthine, as the years have gone by. It has proliferated and convoluted well beyond the grasp of any layman with nothing more than a good general education behind him'[40]. The NCC report describes the main advice services both voluntary and official. Whilst calling for a fairer geographical distribution and better collaboration between agencies, combined with an ability to undertake advocacy as well as advice, it does not attempt to evaluate the quality of service available from different agencies. The joint NCC/ NCSS report on rural advice services[41] attempts some evaluation of differing approaches to delivery of advice and information in rural areas:- evaluation in terms of physical accessibility, and the quality of back-up for advisors, but not the quality of the information and advice given. The field is still wide open for research as to the 'fit' between the advice and information needs of those living in localities with high deprivation indices scores and the services actually provided. The provision of DHSS 'Freefone' and computer information outlets needs careful independent monitoring if a simplistic assumption that provision of information in these forms meets needs is to be open to question. The cost of not knowing, or being given wrong information needs to be evaluated, and although the NCSS/NCC report sees this as a particular problem for country people, the over-lapping boundaries and difficulties of access by public transport to various services were also a concern of the Lambeth Inner Area Study[42]. Despite the existence of a number of information centres in or accessible to its study area population 'on the evidence of the household survey these have not done much to help the considerable number of residents who are ignorant about all kinds of services - rate and rent rebates, housing advice, social services... etc'[42]. This led to the consultants' proposal for a localised referral point to services (a 'local information post'), which, the consultants believed (if it were sufficiently local and sufficiently conspicuous) would make it almost impossible for residents <u>not</u> to get information when necessary. Once again the assumption is that mere provision of a service will meet need and there is no recognition of the constraints imposed by the quality of staff, the advocacy stance which the agency adopts, and the involvement within an agency of people who share the experiences of deprivation of its users. The voluntary sector resource centres, Welfare Rights Information services and Law Centres need similar qualitative assessment, in order to guide resource providers as to the best value for money in the provision of information and advice to areas of deprivation. Good examples of such evaluation are to be found in the CPF study of two urban resource centres[43] and the study of provision of a mobile service in the rural area of Cumbria CDP[44].

Since re-organisation of Local Government in England and Wales many rural areas have seen a decrease in the number of local authority service points at which information is available. This may be particularly important in relation to the take-up of housing benefit, as my research in East Anglia[9] suggests some link between low population density and take-up of rebates in 1972/3, particularly where access to district council offices was poor. Some confirmation of this is to be found in Thomas and Winyard's work in rural Wales[16]. More work comparing take-up in individual settlements measured against an objective accessibility factor is needed.

In the 1980's a vital need is for information about job vacancies. This is a particular problem for the isolated rural unemployed person, who may lack income or transport for speculative visits to Job Centres or potential employers. The use of mobile libraries and village noticeboards to display job vacancies is currently undergoing trial in some rural areas[45]. This process involves Job Centre staff selecting vacancies which they believe to be suitable and runs counter to the 'self-service' philosophy which allows selection from among all the vacancies displayed on Job-Centre boards. Althugh cable TV networks may be able to offer employment information such networks seem unlikely to penetrate rural areas. There is room for evaluative research on the provision of employment information and the penetration of Government Training Schemes such as YTS in rural areas.

Sub-post offices have always been considered as a source of basic information needs, such as benefit leaflets. In rural areas these have been fast disappearing in the smaller settlements, as Packman and Wallace show[46]. In Suffolk in 1978 37 per cent of parishes did not have a post office, and in Norfolk in 1980 28 per cent of parishes containing 40,000 people were without one[46]. A review of urban sub-post offices is now under way, and Holman[47] has chronicled the effect of a closure decision on the residents of a council estate in Bath. Studies of the effect of such closure on benefit take-up and substitute information sources is necessary if the information function of Post Offices is to be used as a factor in the argument for retention of 'uneconomic' outlets.

Lack of information and advice services will affect not only economic well-being, but the exercise of political power; without good information it is all too easy for the exercise of such power to founder when faced with the information available to officials and planners. There are signs of planners becoming sceptical of the usefulness of participation exercises, with their inevitable mixed and sectionally motivated responses, so that the dangers of increasing 'non-decision-making'[48] exist. Newby et al[49] would suggest this is a particular danger in rural areas with a tradition of consensus politics. Yet it is just these areas which have little or no access to independent resource and advice centres. The result is well summed up by a Planning Officer quoted by Buchanan[50] 'The believers in conservation know their rights and know how to speak up. A lot of people don't think this way and would support expansion, but their views aren't represented'.

CONCLUSIONS

It is important to recognise the limitation of the spatial concept of deprivation. It is possible to recognise areas of high concentration of deprivation, which, because of the way data is collected, appear to be found mainly in our inner cities. Yet as Holterman says[7] 'although there is some degree of spatial concentration of deprived people into the "worst" areas, there are large numbers of deprived people who live outside them'. This view is confirmed by Townsend '....even in the poorest group of areas, a quarter of the people interviewed were relatively prosperous, and in the richest areas 14 per cent had incomes around the poverty standard'[3]. Townsend continues 'The majority of the poor are not to be found in areas which even account for 20 per cent of the population; and there are substantial minorities of relatively prosperous people living in the poorest districts of the country'[3].

The proximity of deprived people, the density and visibility of deprivation in some urban areas, lends itself to measurement and description in the tradition of Booth[20][51]. Rural deprivation is both less visible and less proximate. Yet many of the symptoms in housing, employment and incomes are present in significant proportions in small rural areas. In both urban and rural areas marked job loss in traditional primary and manufacturing industries pre-dates the current recession.

Area deprivation policies are often attempting to ameliorate the casualty level caused by major policy trends, or sometimes their unforeseen side effects. Thus Urban Aid and Inner City programmes have taken place alongside planning policies to restrict industrial and population growth in the same areas. The relative post-war prosperity of the retired, with state and occupational pensions has been a contributory factor to geriatric enclaves in rural and sea-side areas with their influence on the availability of housing. In terms of the marginal resources devoted to the various urban programmes it could be argued that post-war policy has supported the idea of decentralisation and that this is a necessary transitional stage before full-scale economic regeneration of the older areas. It is possible to argue that the transitional period involved a price paid by the manual workers in the areas of economic decline, and that it is the political and organisational disadvantage of the working class in these areas that needs to be corrected if they are to influence the regenerative stage. These arguments of powerless-ness are promulgated by the CDP studies in urban areas, and most notably by Newby et al in their studies of the politics of the status quo in East Anglia[49]. Some hope for participation in their future can be gained from such exercises as the 'People's Plan for Dockland' in London[52], but there is little sign in rural areas that the consultation process inherent in submission of Structure Plans is leading to significant participation other than by the conservation lobby[50]. Thus the benefits of the spatial distribution of resources can all too easily accrue to middle-class newcomers or commuters, leaving indigenous working-class people relatively deprived. If such deprivation is to be relieved during what is hopefully a transitional period before economic regeneration, then area poverty cannot be divorced from deprivation and privilege generally. As Lawless concludes in his study of government initiative in urban deprivation[2] 'In terms of actually attempting to reduce day-to-day poverty, as opposed to trying to regenerate urban economic bases, it would be far more sensible to raise supplementary or unemployment benefits nationally. It would be far more effective in reaching those who must be generally regarded as poor'. Yet to do this would involve a redistribution away from the relatively privileged, a process which most post-war governments have been singularly reluctant to embark upon. Hall comments 'Social policy has consisted of squeezing limited extra resources to pay groups that have campaigned the loudest, but in the process no other group must ever sacrifice any of its subsidies or privileges' [53].

Social workers and others whose daily work brings them into direct contact with the deprived have contributed to the marginal, incrementalist nature of anti-deprivation programmes by diluting their energies in a multitude of campaigns and pressure groups, and failing to unite effectively around any agreed priority areas for action. The potential for relief of deprivation that could follow an end of cut-throat competition for resources by different sections of the helping professions, and its replacement by effective campaigning with and on behalf of the poor is enormous. Such a stance is all the more important in an era of 'negative incrementalism' in which a diminishing pool of resources is made available for the relief of deprivation.

References

1. Plowden Report. Children and their Primary Schools. HMSO, 1967.
2. Lawless, P. Urban Deprivation and Government Initiative. Faber, 1979.
3. Townsend, P. Poverty in the United Kingdom. Penguin, 1979.
4. Canning Town CDP. Canning Town to North Woolwich - The Aims of Industry? Canning Town CDP 1975.
5. Liverpool Inner Area Study. Final Report. 'Change or Decay' Dept of Environment. 1977
6. Eversley, D.E.C. 'Old Cities, falling populations and rising costs' G.L.C. Intelligence Unit Quarterly Bulletin. No. 18, March, 1982.
7. Holterman, S. 'Census Indicators of Urban Deprivation' CIUD Working Note. No. 6, DOE, 1975.
8. Holterman, S. 'Areas of Urban Deprivation in Great Britain. An analysis of the 1971 census data' Social Trends. No. 6. HMSO, 1975.
9. Brogden, G. 'A Study of Deprivation in an English Rural District' Unpublished MA dissertation. University of Essex, 1975.

10. Moor, N. 'Jobs in Jeopardy - a study of job prospects in older industrial areas' Report to CDP on behalf of Batley, Benwell, Canning Town and North Shields CDP's. 1974
11. Birmingham CDP 'Workers on the Scrap-heap' Birmingham CDP. 1975.
12. National CDP 'The Costs of Industrial Change' CDP Inter-Project Editorial Team. 1977.
13. Dept of Employment. Employment Gazette. HMSO, January 1984.
14. NCVO. Jobs in the Countryside - prospects for rural employment. NCVO. 26 Bedford Square, London. 1980.
15. I am obliged to the regional office of M.A.F.F. for these figures.
16. Thomas, C. & Winyard, S. 'Rural Incomes' in Shaw, J.M. (Ed.) Rural Deprivation and Planning. Geo. Abstracts 1979.
17. Packman, J. 'Rural Employment - Problems and Planning' in. Shaw, J.M. (Ed.) Rural Deprivation and Planning. Geo. Abstracts, 1979.
18. East Anglia Regional Strategy Team. Strategic Choice for East Anglia. HMSO, 1974.
19. Association of County Councils. 'Rural Areas in England & Wales' Report for A.C.C. by Norfolk County Planning Department. 1979.
20. Harrison, P. Inside the Inner City - Life Under the Cutting Edge. Penguin Books, 1983.
21. Clark, D. 'Rural Housing Problems and Solutions' Housing Review. Nov-Dec 1983, 185-7.
22. Fabes, R. Worsley, L. & Howard, M. The Myth of the Rural Idyll. Leicestershire Child Poverty Action Group. 1983.
23. Clark, D. 'Council House Sales, Rural Safeguards' in Rural Housing Initiatives. N.C.V.O. 26 Bedford Square, London. 1981.
24. Phillips, D. & Williams, A. 'Council House Sales & Village Life' New Society. 25th November 1981, 367-9
25. Clark, D. 'Assessing Hidden Need in the Parishes' in Rural Housing Initiatives. N.C.V.O., 26 Bedford Square, London. 1981.
26. Shucksmith, M. No Homes for Locals. Gower, 1981.
27. Coleman, R. 'Second Homes in North Norfolk' in Moseley, M.J. (Ed.) Power, Planning and People in Rural East Anglia. Centre of East Anglian Studies, U.E.A. Norwich, 1982.
28. Coles, R. 'Retirement in Rural North Norfolk' in Moseley, M.J. (Ed.)
Power, Planning and People in Rural East Anglia. Centre of East Anglian Studies, U.E.A. Norwich, 1982.

29. Figures supplied by Ministry of Agriculture.
30. Dowling, S. Health for a Change. CPAG/NEC, 1983.
31. Black Report. Inequalities in Health. Townsend, P. & Davidson, N. (Eds.) Penguin Books, 1982.
32. Heller, T. 'Health and Health Services' in Walker, A. (Ed.) Rural Poverty. CPAG, 1978.
33. HMSO, General Household Survey, 1971. HMSO, 1972.
34. Rutter, M. & Madge, N. Cycles of Disadvantage. Heinemann, 1976.
35. Sainsbury, P. Suicide in London - An Ecological Study. Oxford University Press, 1955.
36. Shaw, M. & Stockford, D. 'The Role of Statutory Agencies in Rural Areas: Planning and Social Services' in Shaw, J.M. (Ed.) Rural Deprivation and Planning. Geo. Abstracts 1979.
37. Moseley, M.J. Accessibility - The Rural Challenge. Methuen, 1979.
38. Fennell, G., Emerson, A.R., Sidell, M. & Hague, A. Day Centres for the Elderly in East Anglia. Centre for East Anglian Studies, Norwich, 1981.
39. Stockford, D. 'Social Services Provision' in Walker A. (Ed.) Rural Poverty. CPAG, 1978.
40. National Consumer Council. The Fourth Right of Citizenship - A Review of Local Advice Services. N.C.C. 1977.
41. NCC/NCSS The Right to Know - A Review of Advice Services in Rural Areas. Bedford Square Press, 1978.
42. Shankland Cox Partnership. Lambeth Inner Area Study - Interim Report on Local Services. Dept of Environment 1974.
43. Taylor, M. Street Level - Two Resource Centres & Their Users. Community Projects Foundation, 1980.
44. Butcher, H., Cole, I. & Glen, A. Information and Action Services for Rural Areas - A Case Study in Cumbria. Dept of Social Administration & Social Work, University of York. 1975.
45. Community Council for Suffolk. Annual Report, 1982/3. County Hall, Ipswich, 1983.
46. Packman, J. & Wallace, D. 'Rural Services in Norfolk & Suffolk - the Management of Change' in Moseley, M.J. (Ed.) Power Planning and People in Rural East Anglia. Centre of East Anglian Studies, U.E.A. Norwich, 1982.
47. Holman, R. 'Last Post in Southdown' Community Care. No. 499, 16th Feb, 1984.
48. Bachrach, J. & Baratz, M.S. Power and Poverty. O.U.P. 1970.

49. Newby, H. Bell, C. & Saunders, P. Property Paternalism and Power - Class and Control in Rural England. Hutchinson, 1978.
50. Buchanan, S. 'Power & Planning in Rural Areas - Preparation of the Suffolk County Structure Plan' in Moseley, M.J. (Ed.) Power, Planning and People in Rural East Anglia. Centre of East Anglian Studies, U.E.A. Norwich, 1982.
51. Rowland, J. Community Decay. Penguin Books 1973.
52. Newham Docklands Forum. The People's Plan for the Royal Docks. Greater London Council, 1983.
53. Hall, P. 'Introduction' to Issues in Urban Society. Davies, R. & Hall, P. (Eds.) Penguin Books, 1978.

THE RURAL - URBAN DICHOTOMY IN SOCIAL CARE: RHETORIC AND REALITY

Gordon Grant

INTRODUCTION

This chapter has two principal and related aims. The first is to examine the validity of assumptions about rural-urban differences in the provision of social care. The second has to do with the main sources of social care and their inter-relatedness. The main concern therefore lies with the connections between informal, voluntary and formal care in contrasting territorial contexts, and with the implications for the organisation and management of care. Although the chapter is necessarily restricted in length, some international comparisons are drawn where they seem relevant.

INFORMAL CARE

Historical Note

Much of the prevailing debate about the distinctiveness of rural as opposed to urban styles of living has its origins in the history of research into the subject. It is therefore worth setting the scene by briefly considering what we have inherited from early studies.

The early reports of sociologists and social anthropologists have tended to emphasise the cohesiveness, stability and self supporting nature of rural communities[1][2][3]. The images presented in Rees's study of Llanfihangel yng Ngwnfa, for example, leave little doubt about the existence of widespread neighbouring and about the notion of the community functioning as if as a complete social organism.

Such imagery is still popular, and perpetrated perhaps more than anywhere else by ad men seeking to equate their 'products' with the natural charms of the countryside. There are therefore powerful elements, like the media, in present-day society which perpetuate images of an imagined past and their influence is obviously a force to be reckoned with. However the validity of such sets of assumptions about rural life appears to need some drastic reappraisal.

The tendency to equate Tonnies[1] gemeinschaftlich qualities with the countryside and gesellschaftlich features with the city received a considerable jolt following the publication of Young and Willmott's[4] seminal study of family and kinship in Bethnal Green, London. The existence of working class 'villages' in cities led to an altogether different impetus in the search for factors which explain patterns of social relationships. The flurry of studies which followed Young and Willmott's work has tended to suggest that residential instability and degrees of heterogeneity (notably in age, class and race) in the community predispose to the varying intensity of social relations (see Gans[5], Willmott[6], Bell[7], Stacey[8] for example). Moreover, a powerful critique of the earlier community studies has emerged in the writings of Pahl[9] and Bell and Newby[10] who, in different ways, have taken to task the functionalist perspective of those studies which emphasised stability and equilibrium and overlooked wider influences such as power, social change and social stratification in rural communities.

A penetrating historical review by Laslett[11] has also questioned the factual as well as the interpretive basis of assumptions about the widespread existence of the extended family in pre-industrial society. As a result of life-expectancy and custom, few families could hope to survive long enough to see their grand children. Abrams[12] tends to share this view and suggests that most of what we know about community care in rural areas is based on communities which are either doomed to disappear or which we should strongly hope will disappear. In other words, self-help and solidarity in these communities were responses to survival needs rather than to spontaneous expressions of altruism.

Today, therefore, the picture is somewhat confused. Stereotypes based on outdated images still persist, and are even being actively promoted by those with commercial interests. During the 1960's and

1970's the welfare state has mushroomed, social and geographic mobility have increased, and now, in the 1980's, all areas have felt the effects of the recession. How does this leave the capacity of rural and urban areas to care for those who cannot always help themselves? And how valid today are assumptions about rural-urban differences in social care?

Care and the Family

Despite the rhetoric about its supposed decline and its nucleation the family still appears to be the strongest and most reliable source of care in both rural and urban areas. Although the existing knowledge base is still less than comprehensive for making this assertion, research findings are nonetheless persuasive. Sample surveys of the elderly[13] show there to be minimal territorial differences in the supply of family care, and independent studies in urban areas[14] and rural areas[15] only corroborate these unspectacular findings. Indeed, consistent patterns occur in cross-national studies[16]. This source of reassurance comes also from research into the care of mentally handicapped people[17][18][19] in different territories, and from studies of physically handicapped persons[20][21].

Families also show a high degree of adaptability to the needs of dependants. Studies of the elderly and their carers in Leeds[22], Sheffield[23] and North Wales[15] all show that family care arrangements respond to increasing levels of disability and that care of the highly personal and intensive kind is carried out almost exclusively by family members.

From what various studies of the elderly tell us, levels of contact between old people and their families are roughly equivalent in urban and rural communities[13][14][15]. Bultena's study[24] in the U.S. tends to support these findings. Contact, in fact, is the norm and Wenger's rural study[15] goes on to report impressive evidence of the varieties of ways in which family members seek to maintain the security of elderly dependants in spite of the difficulties of travelling distances, terrain and poor rural transport.

Some supporting evidence for this comes from the U.S. in the work of Hynson[25]. He attempted to assess qualitative aspects of intra family ties and apparently discovered that satisfaction with family and community was higher among the elderly living in rural as opposed to urban areas. A hole was later blown through Hynson's work by a re-analysis of the same data by Sauer, Shehan and Boymel [26]. They showed that what at first seemed to be a 'real' rural-urban distinction was due largely to the effects of other intervening variables such as health, marital status, race, income and work status.

This leaves us with a problem. Much of the debate about comparisons between rural and urban areas rests on studies which are not, methodologically, strictly comparable, or on data banks which have not been analysed exhaustively enough to make worthwhile territorial comparisons possible. There is a moral here about development of more replication research conducted deliberately across different territories. In this respect the UK track record leaves something to be desired. Whilst independence in the execution of research is to be valued, there may be mutually beneficial advantages in researchers, and research units, collaborating much more in the interests of properly conducted replication or comparative studies.

This caveat about research management aside, the evidence reported so far does not suggest that rural life is any more benign or appealing than that in urban centres. Having concentrated on some of the more positive aspects of family care and concern, it is now necessary to make some important qualifications.

Although research in rural Wales and mining towns tends to suggest that old people have several people in their social networks, and an extraordinarily large number of contacts that they could name, the function of providing care tends to fall on the shoulders of one, or usually at most two, family members. In short, responsibility for providing the more personal, and therefore critical, forms of care needed to maintain dependants at home falls very unevenly on individual family members, most of it on females as research amply demonstrates[18],[19],[27],[28],[29]. Research has yet to get to grips with ways in which obligations for care might be more equitably distributed, with attendant reduction in stress and anxiety to those most closely involved. At the moment the difficulties in distributing care tasks appear to relate to family and societal expectations of female roles, the significance of intimate and long-standing intra-family ties, the sheer complexity of organising personal care on a more democratic rota basis, or the unwillingness in some members to abrogate their caring roles out of a sense of duty, loyalty or respect.

At the moment we know only a limited amount about the capacity of family care networks to adapt to changing care demands. Moreover, accounts about the management of care reported in the literature usually emanate from dependent subjects or what might be termed the 'main' family carer. We are still devoid of perspectives drawn more directly from grandparents, husbands, siblings, brothers, sisters, aunts, uncles, nephews, nieces and other relatives. Research, to be useful in this sphere of social policy, needs to address questions about how caring relationships are initiated, under what circumstances networks of family care falter, what support carers receive or need to carry on caring, and how decision making systems relate to the successful management of care.

Research is, however, helping to break down stereotypes of the structure of family care. To take the example of the elderly[13][15], we know that a significant number of carers for the elderly are themselves elderly. As many as one in ten of the elderly population are responsible for the care of a handicapped, ill or elderly dependant. Substantial numbers of old people are childless and have attenuated or less diffuse family networks available to them. This type of diversity appears to be common to both rural and urban communities. Similar forms of differentiation in family care occur with respect to other dependency groups such as the mentally handicapped, the mentally ill and the chronic sick, but there is still a lot to know about the coping strategies of different families set against the diversity of need within specific dependency groups. For example, if carers are seen in their context as single parents, widows of divorcees or as persons with obligations towards others besides the main dependant then a whole variety of support structures can be anticipated. Equally, it seems important not to look upon care-giving as unidirectional. So-called dependants also participate in varying degrees in family and community life so in this sense their participation may prove to be a vital means by which family carers are themselves supported. The psychological and sociological dynamics of these different relationships seem to warrant further study.

The ability to recognise and work with the needs and natural helping resources that exist is likely to test the awareness and adaptability of formal agencies everywhere, something recognised by the Barclay Report[30] and also, increasingly, in the international literature on self-help and community care[31][32][33]. This raises important issues about the relationship between formal and informal care and the ability of each to cope with a healthy measure of interdependence on the other. Set against this, the rural-urban issue tends to fade in significance. Later it is argued that different forms of service delivery in rural and urban areas may well emanate from a more effective fusion of formal and informal care resources, but first it is necessary to consider the role played by the neighbourhood in the care system.

Care and the Neighbourhood

If the family provides the most important context for care, then friends and neighbours still play a supportive, if more secondary, role. As searching reviews and bibliographies of the literature have identified, neighbouring can subsume a whole host of activities from intensive, regular personal care freely given, to situations resembling little more than passing contact[12][34][35]. It is therefore facile to talk of neighbouring as if it were some kind of homogeneous resource that exists everywhere, or, for that matter, to assume that people perceive the role and function of friends and neighbours in the same way.

A 'good' neighbour, to use Philip Abrams' description, is defined almost invariably as someone who can be counted on to be at once friendly, helpful and distant. Privacy having been claimed, friendliness and helpfulness can be enacted, he suggests. Many of the aforementioned empirical studies tend to bear this out. Friends and neighbours appear to defer to the family where highly personal care such as bathing, washing or help with toileting is required; in other words, in situations where privacy and regularity are at a premium. However, friends and neighbours are drawn much more into the performance of domestic chores such as shopping and lift-giving, or as trusted sources of support at times of crisis such as acute illness or worry. Frequently, it appears to be easier, or preferable, to seek out the 'friendly ear' of a neighbour rather than confide in close relatives. Interestingly, these patterns are maintained across highly contrasting territories from rural Wales, Birmingham and East Anglia[36], so again the rural-urban dichotomy does not provide the crucial explanatory paradigm.

In some of the mental handicap studies referred to earlier, evidence is reported of efforts by family carers to avoid indebtedness not only to other relatives, but also to friends and neighbours. To a large extent, research appears to have been concerned primarily with asking who is turned to, and for what kind of help. It would now seem to be worth concentrating some effort on understanding the motivational forces behind help seeking activity, and equally, the inhibiting factors that prevent help from being sought from secondary sources in the community.

From much of the work reviewed so far some glimpses can be obtained about why overstretched family carers may decide not to seek care from other sources. Firstly, many of the obligations placed on kin are socially defined so there are strong normative pressures to appear as if you are coping even if you are not. Hence, neighbours, or professionals, may fail to recognise the cloak of competence so erected. Secondly, family carers sometimes talk as if they will elicit unsympathetic attitudes from neighbours and, in any case, neighbours are seen as having obligations of their own[37]. Thirdly, there is a question of elicited support not being value free. Often, carers feel for good reasons that they are not in a position to return help that might be offered by friends or neighbours, so it is not sought in the first place. A useful commentary on the notion of reciprocity has more recently suggested that even this is an over-simplification of processes which are much more subtle and complex [38].

Hence, although surveys tend to emphasise the dominant role played by families, the relative absence of neighbourly care should not be interpreted to mean that the community is 'un-caring'. The real problem appears to reside in the extraordinarily high value that families in western society place on their independence and self-sufficiency[39]. Even if latent care in the community can be tapped and harnessed by formal agencies, a difficult enough task in itself, there appear still to be formidable personal and social barriers to break down before such help is made 'acceptable' to those who need it. A useful review of the complexities raised has been presented by Allan[40].

Whilst Abrams[12] has quite rightly pointed out that religion, race and occupation also provide promising contexts for community care, there has been some dispute about the part played by locality. Set against the influence of migration, high levels of car ownership, and the existence of increasingly sophisticated telecommunications, the argument is that the neighbourhood is less significant as an arena where meaningful social interaction takes place. Nevertheless, evidence tends to fly in the face of such conjecture[23][41] as studies of the elderly suggest that there is a strong link between a person's immediate locality and the supply of care both from relatives and also from friends and neighbours. If these findings are generalisable to different territories across the country, they have important ramifications for the type of knowledge base necessary to build a more complete picture of informal care, and of the service delivery stratagems signposted for agencies. Again this is something which appears to cut across a preoccupation with the rural-urban dichotomy.

If the underlying pattern of differentiation in neighbourly care is similar within both urban and rural areas, what do studies tell us about the intensity of that care across territories? The evidence is rather patchy but nevertheless corroborative. For example, studies of the elderly tend to indicate that greater proportions of elderly people in the most sparsely populated areas receive visits from friends, and more both make and receive calls on their neighbours[13][15]. There is also a suggestion from Wenger's study that higher proportions of the rural elderly get on well with all or most of their neighbours, can ask them favours or have confidants. However, it is important to note that in these studies it is only a small proportion who respond negatively to these questions. Although it is possible to detect some rural-urban differences here, it is important to note that they are differences in degree rather than in kind.

Overall, rural-urban differences in neighbouring patterns are not particularly marked. Research might do well to address why levels and forms of neighbouring can vary so much within specific localities. Although some writers maintain that neighbourhoods can be classified in ways which distinguish their capacity for self-support and care[41] the link between neighbourliness and structural factors still remains unclear. Smaller scale studies which make greater use of ethnography would seem to have a role to play here. Certainly, studies at the level of 'the street'[43] appear to have the capacity to explain more clearly how dependency relationships and interdependencies emerge and this seems a fruitful line of further investigation. Equally, commentators have argued forcibly for research to concentrate on the circumstances which make it possible for some social relationships which start out as no more than social contact to transform themselves into situations where the exchange of care is possible[12][40]. A useful start has already been made in developing a taxonomy of neighbouring[44] which might pave the way for further study in this area.

ORGANISED VOLUNTARY CARE

If family and neighbour relationships fail to throw up dramatic differences between rural and urban contexts, what about evidence of participation in voluntary groups and of the supply and distribution of voluntary organisation activity?

Perhaps the only study to have looked at the territorial distribution of voluntary organised care was that concerning good neighbour schemes in England[45]. Schemes were found to be least common in established middle income areas and stable low income areas and most common in those areas of noticeable social heterogeneity. Although schemes were found in all conceivable types of area, there was no simple correlation between their prevalence, the probable supply of helpers and the existence of need. Distributionally, their existence did not reflect hints of real rural-urban differences. Though hidden factors may be at work in determining how and where these schemes develop, hypotheses surrounding the link between their emergence and the decline, or absence, of informal care, would be interesting to explore further. Equally, the disadvantaged position of certain areas in the supply of statutory services may have something to do with the availability of voluntary care schemes of this type. What remains true is that we know relatively little about the support and survival needs of these extended modes of care, wherever they exist.

The only other survey of this type into voluntary organisation activity is yet to produce its findings[46]. The Wales Council for Voluntary Action has already completed a survey of voluntary organisations throughout Wales, and is now in the process of cataloguing factors which relate to variations in the supply and organisation of a wide range of voluntary action, and to the categories of need which they seek to meet.

There have been one or two comparable studies which have investigated patterns of participation by different consumer groups in voluntary organisations. For example, if we compare the findings of Wenger and Hunt about the elderly[13][15] it would seem that some interesting rural-urban differences do in fact emerge. In spite of reduced opportunities which result from distance and lack of transport, elderly people in rural areas appear more likely to belong to voluntary bodies, to be in contact with religious institutions, to attend meetings and to engage in spare time activities which provide potential for contact with others. In short, the level of integration within the community seems to be higher than in urban samples. There appear to be several explanations for this.

Voluntary groups and religious bodies are, first of all, not only more visible in rural communities; they are frequently the only source of organised diversion or entertainment available. Moreover, there is often considerable overlap between church, or chapel, and voluntary associations. There is also a suggestion that the environment itself directly affects the scope of spare time activities. The attraction of walking and gardening in rural areas for example takes people outdoors and into contact with others. This may reflect less an intrinsic interest in the activities themselves and more an expression of the security which the elderly seem to feel in an environment where they are known to many people around them, and where anxieties about crime, vandalism and environmental pollution do not arise. The position of groups other than the elderly is less clear since there is so little published material, making direct comparison impossible.

Also, there has been no attempt so far, it would seem, to analyse and compare the activities of Rural Community Councils and their urban counterparts, Councils of Voluntary (or Social) Service, to see whether distinctive patterns of voluntary sector organisation prevail. These councils obviously have a vital part to play in the launching of community and social care initiatives[47]. Their ability to act as effective intermediaries between central government and local voluntary action would seem to depend on their ability to be trusted by those who wish to promote development and those who are, or could be, directly engaged in local voluntary action. Although this raises a whole complex of issues[48][49], one that directly concerns us here is their link to the local state, notably the statutory social services.

From the few studies reviewed here it is difficult to draw generalisations. There would seem to be value for future research to ask questions less about the prevalence of voluntary organised action, and more about the form it takes and the significance it has in the lives of ordinary people. From anecdotal remarks in some studies it is possible to obtain glimpses of how new friendships can emerge from participation in a shared community of interest such as a voluntary body. Multiplier effects stemming from this type of linkage have therefore been acknowledged. What is now needed is a more detailed understanding of the social processes which allow meaningful social relationships to be developed in this way. Equally the reasons why many people do not join voluntary organisations of one kind or another are not well understood. As voluntary and statutory bodies consider moves towards working partnerships in the field of social care, there must be fears in some quarters that this will lead to greater formalisation of existing arrangements. Whether this will act as an incentive or disincentive for people to join or remain inactive in voluntary groups remains to be seen.

FORMAL CARE

So far there have only been hints at how professionals and their agencies organise themselves to deal with presenting rural and urban needs, and how they relate to other sources of care in the community.

Underpinning the concern of those emphasising the need for special or unique solutions to rural needs has been recognition of declining public services and amenities. This has been amply described in relation to primary schools, doctors' surgeries, chemists, food shops, information services, garage, transport and leisure services in addition to a long list of other amenities[50][51][52][53][54]. By the end of the 1970's the thesis of 'rural deprivation' was well established (see Brogden in this volume). Interwoven with this concern were fears that prevailing models of welfare organisation prevented rural needs from being taken into account. Though much of this impetus came from the U.S.[55][56], there were at least signs in the UK that centralist approaches left something to be desired [57][58].

Although there can be no doubt about the objective reality of missing public services in many rural communities, the evidence for the 'felt' impact on consumers is a different story. In the U.S., it has been reported that satisfaction with a range of community services in rural Illinois does not increase as a simple linear function of service availability, even after controlling for intervening socio-economic variables[59]. A North Carolina study [60], while reporting a strong link between county population densities and community perceptions of service availability, did not show anything like the same association when examining questions about the quality of services. Other studies in the US show that the utilisation of physicians does not depend at all on geographical factors when important intervening variables such as health, income, attitudes and demography are taken into account[61]. Similar findings emerged in a study of hospital services in West Norfolk where only minimal differences were found in the satisfaction expressed by people living in 'accessible' and 'inaccessible' villages[62]. A major review of this and a mass of other evidence of this type suggests that rural service markets are complex, that rural persons regularly travel for health and social services to sources that are preferred, and that community norms also play a large role in determining utilisation patterns and attitudes[63].

These findings raise important issues. First 'objective' deprivation measured by missing formal services should not be taken as a measure of need. Second, those who plan services appear to need to understand, and take into account, the styles of adaptation that typify the local culture. Failure to do so might undermine established systems of coping and create undue dependency on the central or local state. The problem is that an emphasis on integrating formal and informal care has to be balanced against the values of universalism and equity in the way statutory resources are allocated. Third, if it is not already obvious, the rural deprivation thesis has perhaps been overplayed. More seriously, it has masked important issues about how formal services can serve local communities, and about how different sources of care can be more effectively interwoven without undermining local control and accountability.

How do rural and urban social services teams stand up to these challenges? Although empirical studies of teams are still relatively rare they do nevertheless provide some insights into the issues at stake here. The only study which has directly compared rural and urban practice[36] in the UK has shown that there are a wide range of common influences which tend to create responses which are partial and inflexible. if uniform. Interventions and service delivery stratagems showed a striking degree of similarity in each of the teams observed. There were common concerns too. Social workers in all the teams studied felt they needed more delegated authority to work in ways they would have preferred. Greater control over budgets and more determination over the division of labour and organisation of teams were two major considerations. Resources were managed for workers by administrators and local councillors whom they rarely saw. Thus they had little flexibility or scope about how to 'fine tune' resources in line with local needs. Added to this they were subject to systems of management which directed more than they enabled, and which induced conformism. A critical dilema was that innovation and calculated risk taking, even at the level of the individual case, might expose the frailty of professional or agency practice and so threaten the status quo. A tendency to accede to professional and agency norms was therefore witnessed, much in line with what had earlier been reported in the U.S.[64][65]. In short, the more adaptive services which front-line workers were seeking to provide were thwarted to a large degree by the inability to reconcile bureaucratic authority and professional discretion. These problems are hardly new. However, they are at the core of important challenges facing social workers, and their managers, in many parts of the country, as extensive surveys tell us[66].

Social workers appear to be equivocal about mobilising informal care, but for different sets of reasons. In the Black et al study[36], the team operating in an economically marginal area of rural Wales perceived informal care networks as something brittle which professional intervention might destroy, even though many communities were seen as 'self supporting'. In a rural area with a rapidly expanding population, an East Anglian team were ambiguous about the nature and strength of informal care. The seeds of doubt were sufficient to neutralise inclinations towards interweaving. A third team, operating in the heart of an urban conurbation, adjudged that informal care was altogether lacking on newer council estates. Here, mobilisation of care was considered to need a more concerted community work approach. However, this was felt to be impractical with the present level of referral bombardment on the team. Hence, even when territorial differences are perceived, factors combined to produce a common response which understandably sought to reduce risks to a minimum.

Most studies of social work acknowledge the primacy that workers place on casework rather than group or community work approaches, and indeed this is a vital source of job satisfaction and security[66]. Although this may lead workers to privatise their activities[36], there are now strong pressures within the profession for workers to demonstrate their ability to operate independently after the completion of professional training. Status, in short, will come to those who achieve this. One might ask: 'but at what cost to teamwork?'. Teamwork, in the sense of 'a group of people coming together to coordinate activities to prescribed goals'[67], appears to be rare even though it was Seebohm who first suggested establishment of locally based teams as the primary means of providing comprehensive family and community based services and support. Today, models for teamwork are still largely untested. Neither has there been a concerted effort to assess the impact of alternative systems of management on teamwork approaches, and perhaps more importantly, to extend this to consider the impact of teamwork models on clients and community. The tensions embedded in teamwork are not difficult to appreciate however.

Status differences between qualified or unqualified workers, or formal divisions of labour by client group, or blending of fieldwork, residential, day care and voluntary workers may make workers anxious to protect or conserve their position. In short, proposals for teamwork could be seen as eroding professional autonomy[36]. Put another way, teamwork would seem to require 'an atmosphere of openness, adventure, trust, support and a tolerance for ambiguity'[68]. From the available evidence local authority social services departments do not have a good track record in achieving these conditions[36][66][69][70]. To this extent there must therefore exist fears about the possibilities for creative social work, and community social work in particular.

Acting as gatekeepers for clients to a variety of agencies, social workers, for their effective performance, depend on a high degree of cooperation from other professionals as well as other statutory and voluntary bodies. Although inter-agency activity is common when it comes to referring cases, it seldom appears to develop into coordinated plans for action either in rural or urban areas[36]. The reasons seem to lie beyond notions of role uncertainty and ill-designed structures. They appear to stem from different professional and lay constructions and perceptions of the work, and imbalances in power and status between the various groups involved.

If we accept a second assumption embedded in the idea of teamwork, namely 'to overcome the disadvantages of specialisation by improving coordination'[67], then multidisciplinary teams may yet lead to more balanced views of 'whole person' care. The key seems to lie in recognising interdependencies between the professions, and agencies, and in accepting that no single discipline has a monopoly of expertise in dealing with community care needs. This interpretation would see professional hegomony and community care as inimical, but are practitioners in the field ready to accept this? Cherished professional values may have to be jettisoned if we want to get right our assessment of need, our evaluations of care networks, our plans for coordinated action, and our procedures for accountability. These issues are no more unique to workers in rural areas than to their counterparts in urban areas.

DISCUSSION

Throughout this chapter it has been argued that the key challenges facing those with an interest in developing social care are essentially the same in both rural and urban areas. The issues at stake have little to do with the supposed rural-urban dichotomy. They are part of wider debates about the balance between family, community and state intervention; the equation between consumer participation, choice or sovereignty and professional expertise; and the building of structures which promote participative democracy and which serve rather than service the community.

Arguably, if services and support systems are to be at all adaptive to community needs, there would seem to be a need to relate team structures and teamwork to sets of priorities which reflect local needs and conditions. This would mean leaving behind old debates about genericism versus specialism or patch versus non-patch approaches. Simply put, agencies would be faced with the possibility of variations in the organisation of locally based teams, depending on the needs and conditions in each locality.

Sensitive interweaving of formal and informal care would require a move away from narrow notions of individual casework to activities which also embrace brokerage, entrepreneurial and organisational skills. Fortunately there are now some concrete examples about how these roles can be operationalised to good effect[23][71][72]. Since it is unlikely that any one individual will possess all the requisite skills, it seems that authority and responsibility for pursuing these tasks might be best vested in locally based multi-disciplinary teams. They would probably be entrusted with their own budgets so that decisions concerning the transformation of cash into service are made by those with the most detailed knowledge of each locality or case. In these respects, teams might begin to embody the delegated authority which advocates of patch systems put forward [73][74], with micro-budgeting techniques which are at the root of rationalist approaches[75] and neighbourhood approaches which are trying to tease out the different forms which interweaving might take[23]. The manning and budget levels required to accomplish these tasks are matters requiring further attention.

Nevertheless these elements would go some way towards providing incentives for front-line workers to adapt and change their activities since there are strong suggestions that these represent preferred ways of working[30]. Such changes beg questions about the leadership qualities required of team managers. More fundamentally, they question the willingness of elected representatives and senior managers to operate in a participative system where political control and the management of resources are more open to scrutiny by consumers and by the general public. This, perhaps, is the greatest challenge for here lies a quite explicit challenge to the established bureaucratic order. The organisational and legislative context of social work exerts an extremely powerful influence over the direction and scope for professional endeavour[36][76], and it is difficult to envisage widespread change without a strong and equally widespread commitment of political will.

At the same time, there remain substantial edifices to overcome in promoting partnerships between different statutory and voluntary agencies. Much of the debate in the literature has been on the willingness and commitment of the statutory sector to embrace the voluntary sector, but one is left to question whether voluntary bodies would be willing partners. For what price can their independence and tradition be bought in the interest of a collectivist enterprise? Indeed there remain vital questions at the root of what type of collectivism should be offered. Equally, the inertia and resistance generated by varied ideological conceptions and status differences between professionals should not lightly be dismissed. If inroads cannot be made in this area, services in rural and urban areas run the risk of remaining fragmented and uncoordinated.

If these sorts of major challenges can be faced and overcome, there is a chance that formal services may turn out to be more adaptive and effective. The creative possibilities for social work outreach, para-professional involvement, mobile service delivery, carer relief and community development are endless. The forms they take, in an adaptive system, would therefore reflect their acceptability and legitimacy to the community. Experimentation would obviously be one way forward, backed preferably by political, bureaucratic, professional and voluntary sector will. The likelihood is that outcomes will once and for all obliterate the rural-urban divide. The dichotomy is misleading and over simplistic. It is also dangerous for it deflects attention away from challenging questions about the relationship between different sources of social care and how these might best be related to social and community need.

References and Notes

1. Tonnies, F. Gemeinschaft und Gesellschaft. Harper, New York. 1957.
2. Redfield, R. The Little Community. University of Chicago Press, Chicago. 1956.
3. Rees, A. Life in a Welsh Countryside. University of Wales Press, Cardiff. 1950.
4. Young, M. & Willmott, P. Family and Kinship in East London. Penguin Books, Harmondsworth. 1962.
5. Gans, H. The Levittowners: Ways of Life and Politics in a New Suburban Community. Penguin Books, Harmondsworth. 1967.
6. Willmott, P. The Evolution of a Community: A Study of Dagenham After Forty Years. Routledge and Kegan Paul, London. 1963.
7. Bell, C. Middle Class Families. Routledge and Kegan Paul, London. 1968.
8. Stacey, M. Tradition and Change: A Study of Banbury. University Press, Oxford. 1960.
9. Pahl, R. E. Urbs in Rure. Weidenfeld and Nicolson, London. 1965.
10. Bell, C. & Newby, H. Community Studies. Allen and Unwin, London. 1971.
11. Laslett, P. The World We Have Lost. Matthew & Co., London. 1965.
12. Abrams, P. 'Community Care: Some Research Problems and Possibilities' in Barnes, J. & Connelly, N. Social Care Research. Bedford Square Press, London. 1977, 78-103.
13. Hunt, A. The Elderly at Home: A Study of People Aged Sixty-five and Over Living at Home in England in 1976. Office of Population Censuses and Surveys, London, 1978.
14. Abrams, M. Beyond Three Score and Ten: A Report on a Survey of the Elderly. Age Concern, London, 1977.
15. Wenger, G. C. The Supportive Network: Coping with Old Age. Allen and Unwin, London. In press.

16. Shanas E., Townsend, P., Wedderburn, D., Friss, H., Milhoj, P. & Stehouver, J. Old People in Three Industrial Societies. Atherton Press, New York. 1968.
17. Bayley, M. Mental Handicap and Community Care. Routledge and Kegan Paul, London 1973.
18. Wilkin, D. Caring for the Mentally Handicapped Child. Croom Helm, London. 1979.
19. Glendinning, C. Unshared Care: Parents and their Disabled Children. Routledge and Kegan Paul, London, 1983.
20. Harris, A. Handicapped and Impaired in Great Britain. HMSO, London, 1971.
21. Buchanan, J. The Mobility of Disabled People in a Rural Environment. The Royal Association for Disability and Rehabilitation, 1982.
22. Johnson, M., Di Gregorio, S. & Harrison, B. Ageing, Needs and Nutrition. Policy Studies Institute, London, 1982.
23. Bayley, M., Seyd, R., Tennant, A. & Simons, K. What Resources Does The Informal Sector Require to Fulfil its Role? Paper presented to NISW seminar on the Barclay Report. Department of Sociological Studies, University of Sheffield, 1981.
24. Bultena, G. L. 'Rural-Urban Differences in the Familial Interaction of the Aged' Rural Sociology. 34, 1969, 5-15.
25. Hynson, L. 'Rural-Urban Differences in Satisfaction Amongst the Elderly' Rural Sociology. 40, 1976, 64-66.
26. Sauer, W., Shehan, C. & Boymel, C. 'Rural-Urban Differences in Satisfaction Amongst the Elderly: a Re-analysis' Rural Sociology. 41, 1976, 269-275.
27. Nissel, M. & Bonnerjea, L. Family Care of the Handicapped Elderly: Who Pays? Policy Studies Institute, London, 1982.
28. Finch, J. & Groves, D. 'Community Care and the Family: a Case for Equal Opportunities' Journal of Social Policy. 9, 4, 1980, 487-511.
29. Equal Opportunities Commission. The Experience of Caring for Elderly and Handicapped Dependants. Manchester, 1980.
30. Barclay Report. Social Workers: Their Role and Tasks. Bedford Square Press, London, 1982.
31. Pancoast, D., Parker, P. & Froland, C. Rediscovering Self-Help: its Role in Social Care. Sage Publications, Beverly Hills, 1983.
32. Gourash, N. 'Help Seeking: A Review of the Literature' American Journal of Community Psychology. 6, 1978, 413-425.

33. Collins, A. & Pancoast, D. Natural Helping Networks: A Strategy for Prevention. National Association of Social Workers, Washington DC., 1976.

34. Robinson, F. & Abrams, P. What We Know About the Neighbours: A Working Paper. Rowntree Research Unit, University of Durham, 1977.

35. Robinson, F. & Robinson, S. Neighbourhood Care: An Exploratory Bibliography. The Volunteer Centre, London, 1981.

36. Black, J., Bowl, R., Burns, D., Critcher, C., Grant., G. & Stockford, R. Social Work in Context: A Comparative Study of Three Social Services Teams. Tavistock Publications, London, 1983.

37. Jaehnig, W. Mentally Handicapped Children and Their Families: Problems for Social Policy. Ph.D. Thesis, University of Essex, 1974.

38. Leat, D. Analysing Reciprocity. Policy Studies Institute, London, 1982.

39. Slater, P.E. The Pursuit of Loneliness: American Culture at Breaking Point. Beacon Press, Boston, 1970.

40. Allan, G. 'Informal Networks of Care: Issued Raised by Barclay' British Journal of Social Work. 13, 1983, 417-433.

41. Butcher, H. & Crosbie, D. Pensioned Off: A Study of the Needs of Elderly People in Cleator Moor. Department of Social Administration, University of York, Papers in Community Studies No. 15, 1977.

42. Warren, D.I. 'Support Systems in Different Types of Neighbourhoods' in Garbarino, J. & Stocking, H. Protecting Children from Abuse and Neglect. Jossey Bass, San Francisco, 1980.

43. Bytheway, W. Care in the Street. University College of Wales, Swansea, 1979.

44. Ball, C. & Ball, M. What the Neighbours Say: A Report on a Study of Neighbours. The Volunteer Centre, 1982.

45. Abrams, P., Abrams, S., Humphrey, R. & Snaith, R. Action for Care: A Review of Good Neighbour Schemes in England. The Volunteer Centre, London, 1981.

46. The Wales Council for Voluntary Actions has conducted a census and sample survey of voluntary organised activity throughout Wales. The findings are due for publication towards the end of 1984.

47. Williams, G. 'Community Development in Rural Britain: The Organisation of Local Initiative' Community Development Journal. 14, 2, 1979, 107-114.

48. Wolfenden Report. The Future of Voluntary Organisations. Croom Helm, London, 1978.

49. Griffiths, H. The Development of Local Voluntary Action. Volunteer Centre, NCVO and Home Office, London, 1981.

50. Standing Conference of Rural Community Councils. The Decline of Rural Services. National Council of Social Service, 1978.

51. Moseley, M., Harman, R., Coles, O. & Spencer, M. Rural Transport and Accessibility, Vols. I and II. Centre of East Anglian Studies, University of East Anglia, 1977.

52. Association of County Councils. Rural Deprivation: An A.C.C. Study, 1978.

53. Child Poverty Action Group. Rural Poverty: Poverty, Deprivation and Planning in Rural Areas. London, 1978.

54. Shaw, J. M. Rural Deprivation and Planning. Geo. Abstracts, Norwich, 1979.

55. Ginsberg, L. Social Work in Rural Communities. Council of Social Work Education, New York, 1976.

56. Green, R. & Webster, S. Social Work in Rural Areas: Preparation and Practice. School of Social Work, University of Tennessee, Knoxville, 1976.

57. Hadley, R. & Hatch, S. Social Welfare and the Failure of the State: Centralised Social Services and Participatory Alternatives. Allen & Unwin, London, 1981.

58. Nissel, M., Maynard, A., Young, K. & Ibsen, M. The Welfare State: Diversity and Decentralisation. Discussion Paper No. 2. Policy Studies Institute, London, 1980.

59. Rojek, D., Clemente, F. & Summers, G. 'Community Satisfaction: A Study of Contentment with Local Services' Rural Sociology. 40, 2, 1975, 177-192.

60. Chistensen, J. 'Quality of Community Services: A Macro Dimensional Approach with Experimental Data' Rural Sociology. 41, 4, 1976, 509-525.

61. Luft, H., Hershey, J. & Morrell, J. 'Factors Affecting the Use of Physician Services in a Rural Community' American Journal of Public Health. 66, 9, 1976, 865-871.

62. Haynes, R., Bentham, C., Spencer, M. & Spratley, J. 'Community Attitudes Towards the Accessibility of Hospitals in West

Norfolk' in Moseley, M. J. Social Issues in Rural Norfolk. Centre of East Anglian Studies, University of East Anglia, 1978.

63. Kretz, S.A. An Exploration of the Rural Health Paradigm: The Dilemma of Low Patient Usage of Sponsored Rural Physician Practices. Doctoral Dissertation, Brandeis University, Massachusetts, 1980.

64. Billingsley, A. 'Bureaucratic and Professional Orientation Patterns in Social Casework' Social Service Review. 38, 1964, 400-407.

65. Green, A. 'The Professional Social Worker in the Bureaucracy' Social Service Review. 40, 1966, 71-83.

66. Stevenson, O. & Parsloe, P. Social Services Teams: The Practitioner's View. HMSO, London, 1978.

67. Webb, A. & Hobdell, M. 'Coordination and Teamwork in the Health and Social Services' in Londsdale, S., Webb, A. & Briggs, T. Teamwork in the Personal Social Services and Health Care. Croom Helm, London, 1980.

68. Briggs, T. 'Obstacles to Implementing the Team Approach in Social Services Agencies' in Lonsdale, S., Webb, A., & Briggs, T. Teamwork in the Personal Social Services and Health Care. Croom Helm, London, 1980.

69. Brenton, M. 'Worker Participation and the Social Services Agency' British Journal of Social Work. 8, 3, 1978, 289-300.

70. Glastonbury, B., Cooper D. & Hawkins, P. Social Work in Conflict: The Practitioner and the Bureaucrat. Croom Helm, London, 1980.

71. Challis, D. & Davies, B. 'A New Approach to Community Care of the Elderly' British Journal of Social Work. 10, 1980, 1-18.

72. Grant, G. & Wenger, G.C. 'Patterns of Partnership: Three Models of Care for the Elderly' in Pancoast, D., Parker, P. & Froland, C. Rediscovering Self-Help: Its Role in Social Care. Sage International, London, 1983.

73. Hadley, R. & McGrath, M. Going Local: Neighbourhood Social Services. National Council for Voluntary Organisations, London, 1981.

74. Currie, R. & Parrott, B. A Unitary Approach to Social Work: Application in Practice. BASW, Birmingham, 1981.

75. Davies, B. & Challis, D. 'A Production Relations Evaluation of the Meeting of Needs in the Community Care Projects' in Goldberg, E. M. & Connelly, N. Evaluative Research in Social Care. Heinemann Educational Books, London, 1981.

76. Hallett, C. The Personal Social Services and Local Government. Routledge and Kegan Paul, London, 1982.

IN SEARCH OF COMMON PRINCIPLES IN RURAL SOCIAL AND COMMUNITY WORK

Emilia E. Martinez-Brawley

INTRODUCTION

In discussing current British and North American rural social work developments my intention is to enlighten the decisions of practitioners on both sides of the Atlantic when considering the solutions open to them. The comparisons presented are not an exhaustive analysis of variables but rather observations about rurality in Britain and the U.S. and the principles upon which social and community workers seem to be currently structuring their practices.

Rural generic and generalist practice (including the relationship between community and rural social work) and locality-specific practice (localism) are chosen for examination. While other principles may have been more important at other times, currently conservative governments have caused rural managers to focus more on very concrete pragmatic issues than on broad social causes. The discussion here attempts to be responsive to current practice needs.

SOME COMMENTS ON 'RURAL' IN THE NORTH AMERICAN CONTEXT

The term rural is recognised to be phenomenological. It is characterised by both perceptual ambivalence and demographic uncertainty. On the one hand, rural has been associated with all that is good, uncomplicated and pure; on the other hand, it has also been used to indicate backwardness, undeveloped infrastructures and inability to move with progress.

Ambivalent and contradictory public perceptions of rural have existed and persist in Britain and America, highlighting a common problem that must be contended with by service providers. For, as Newby has suggested, these perceptions, either positive or negative, act as filters through which:

> 'The reality of rural life for those who live in it is constantly being reinterpreted by the rest of society until the stage has been reached where an entirely misleading account of the nature of rural social relationships is believed, not only by those outside, but by those who experience them at first hand[1].

There are other misconceptions surrounding the term rural in the U.S. Here, we will only mention two: individualism and white Anglo-Saxon protestantism, WASP. Not all rural America is composed of 'rugged-individualists', and not all rural America is necessarily WASP.

This recently acknowledged ethnic heterogeneity has permitted the application of the 'internal colonialist' model of analysis to rural America which explains the relationship of 'core', industrial areas, to the non-industrial 'periphery', not only in terms of economic factors but also in terms of the ethnic composition of the latter. In the U.K. this point is illustrated by the long-standing problems of relationships between the mining regions of Wales and Scotland and the core areas of England[2]. The theme of geographic concentration of 'disadvantage' among children also appears in studies by Essen and Wedge[3]. In addition, recent occurrences related to oil exploitation in the North Sea have made the problem even more poignant[4][5][6][7]. In the U.S. examples of the internal colonialist thesis are found in the relationship between highly rural or extractive states (e.g. Vermont, or West Virginia) and the financing centres of the core[8][9].

The placing of particular rural regions within the 'core' or the 'periphery' is important because Government and voluntary responses in the personal social services of the rural areas have been closely determined by the relative power of given rural constituencies. In addition, the self-perception of individuals and the collective image of groups have been crucial in determining the degree of confidence and assertiveness with which rural dwellers have been capable of identifying and expressing their needs and stating their demands.

The study of rural social problems cannot be divorced from the understanding of

1. the economic history of the particular rural area and its relationship to the core;
2. the ethnic composition of the area as it related to the status of particular groups vis-a-vis the economically dominant majority; and
3. the public perceptions and moods which affect firstly, the demands of the grass roots, secondly, the decisions of the policy makers, and thirdly, the degree to which service providers respond to the identified needs of various constituencies.

The diversity which these three considerations imply is well illustrated by Abramson with reference to Canada[10].

> 'When we talk about rural areas we may be thinking about very different kinds of places. For example, we may be picturing a fishing village in Newfoundland, a mining community in northern Quebec or Labrador, a forest based community in New Brunswick, a dry land farming service centre in Saskatchewan, a ranching community in southwestern Alberta, a resort centre in the Canadian Rockies, a fruit growing area in central British Columbia, or a remote native settlement in the Western Northlands'.

For the purpose of this discussion the term rural will be used to describe non-metropolitan areas that are not adjacent to large population centres (since the suburban fringe takes on the infrastructural and socio-cultural characteristics of the contiguous metropolitan area) and which retain the socio-political characteristics ascribed to 'Gemeinschaft'.

What does this mean for the rural resident and the practitioner? Particularly in rural settlements, whether mining towns or agricultural villages, Jordan has suggested that what it means for the resident is simple[11]:

> 'What it amounts to is that a small town resident trades his privacy for understanding and sympathy. And for gossip. Maybe it's sympathetic gossip - and maybe it's not so sympathetic - but it is still gossip'.

The practitioner trades anonimity for mutuality and neighbourliness [12][13].

These are important considerations because many policy analysts and practitioners (particularly those who propose strong locally-based approaches to social work problems) recognise the importance of cohesive and strong informal ties of rural settlements[14][15] where these exist, wonder at their potential for enhancement and problem resolution, while worrying about the danger these strong informal ties pose in perpetuating exclusionary and other undesirable local practices[16]. For there is more to this kind of community than styles of communication or patterns of relationship. Power is likely to be more centralised[17], power actors are likely to have broader and more intertwined spheres of action than in the urban areas and decision making is likely to be more elitist and controlled[18]. In relation to the pyramidal distribution of power in the rural areas, British and American observers again tend to agree, at least on the descriptive level, if not always on the causal explanations. These similarities constituted important bases for the discussions of principles of rural social and community work in two countries.

A recent phenomenon that has caused the revision of many previously held theories of rurality must be mentioned here; recent nostalgic revival has caused rural population and concomitant growth. In the U.S. the trend is undebatable given the results of the 1980 Census which has documented that 'for the first time since 1820 rural areas and small towns are growing faster than the nation's metropolitan areas. The growth in some sections is occurring at a rate more pronounced than demographers expected when the turnaround in migration patterns was detected in the mid-1970s'[19]. The recent rural growth has been not just a demographic but a cultural and social trend and might radically change the nature of many traditional communities[20].

PRINCIPLES OF RURAL SOCIAL WORK

The principles of rural social work selected for comment here are not stated as variables in the empirical sense but rather as philosophic hypotheses revealed through the examination of the U.S. rural social work literature and tested for cross-cultural validity in two prior studies [21][22].

Unfortunately, cross-national comparisons in rural social work in the U.S. literature are scarce, although Canadian scholars and practitioners have often applied an implicit US/Canada comparative perspective in their writings (see for example, the edited collection by Shera[23]) and some have even focused on the similarity of value conflicts between the Scottish and the Canadian oil-related growth of small villages[20].

The focus in this paper, however, is not so much the cross-cultural comparisons but rather the practice issues that seem to commonly concern service providers and managers in the UK and North America.

GENERIC AND GENERALIST PRACTICE IN THE RURAL AREAS

It is important to differentiate between genericism and generalist practice. Both principles have been theoretically favoured as appropriate in rural service delivery in the U.S. and Canada[24[[25] [26].

Yet, there continues to be confusion between the two and the terms are often used interchangeably, particularly in the British literature.

Genericism

Genericism refers to an approach to delivery that does not artifically differentiate the needs of a client according to pre-established 'fields' of professional practice, i.e. it involves the integration of practice across fields, at least at the initial or entry stages of a client into the social work system.

In the U.K. the reorganisation of the social services after Seebohm (1968) and the Scottish Social Work Act (1968) made it not only plausible but mandatory that social work be provided by generic departments. While current descriptions give a more realistic and less idealised image of the generic social service departments (SSDs)[27], SSDs are probably the best settings to put generic (rural or urban) practice in action.

In my study[22] although all of the teams visited were 'generic teams' in the sense that they provided all social work services, not all were 'generic' if the term is applied to the tasks of each individual worker. Some area teams seemed to prefer to have workers assigned to a geographic area within which the worker carried, in most instances, generic responsibilities: e.g. Salisbury area team in Wiltshire. Some geographic area team offices or sub-offices were organised and referred to as 'patches'[28][29]. On the other hand, there were teams where the workers were not assigned to specific local areas or patches: e.g. Glyndwr, Wales. This team provided the 'single door' entry into the system, but did not favour a patch system and workers did have 'fields' of preference or expertise. Workers often spent considerable time driving to localities and appeared, by and large, to prefer that pattern.

In discussion in 1980, rural teams focussed on the workers' disenchantment with genericism. The feeling was that in order for workers to survive and become well-informed, they needed to concentrate on a primary area of interest. Fields of interest were generally defined in terms of particular populations: e.g. the elderly, the blind, etc. Dialogues in many English and Scottish authorities suggested that the tendency was back to some degree of specialisation by field within the existing generic departments and teams.

Because the structure of the personal social services in the U.S. varies greatly from state to state, and because even the so called 'public' services are sponsored by various funding sources and shared between the public and the voluntary sector through 'purchase-of-care' arrangements, services in the U.S. tend to be much more field oriented, fragmented and less generic than in the U.K. Some rural states have experimented with multi-service (multi-field) delivery locations, which, in fact, represent attempts at developing generic departments or 'single door' models of entry into the system[30] but those attempts, have been largely experimental, completely voluntary on the part of counties or states and to this day, rather uncommon. While the rural literature has recommended genericism, rural genericism has been hard to operationalise in the U.S. and has been much more prevalent in Britain.

Generalism

Generalist practice (unitary practice in the U.K.) implies an integrated methodological approach to micro and macro targets and refers to workers who intervene at all levels of the system.

> 'Generalist practice requires a worker to enable individuals families, small groups and larger social systems to promote the best possible relationship between people and their environment' [31].

The rural generalist which the rural social work literature in the U.S. has tended to describe is, using U.K. terminology, a social and community worker all in one. The rural generalist is seen as a supporter of local level organisation and innovation, and a political force in the community that he/she serves[32][33][34].

It is not that generalism per se is different in rural and urban areas. It is that because of factors in the context, generalism is often a must in servicing remote areas while it might be a choice in urban ones.

> 'Generalist practitioners are needed who can specialise by a particular delivery system area and in relation to rural systemic dynamics. In rural areas the community is more clearly defined geographically than in urban settings and where relationships are both visible and susceptible to scientific scrutiny, a practice approach focused on the totality of the community and containing an inherent focus on enhancement of the quality of life is possible'[35].

The rural client's problems are viewed as a result of the problems and short-comings of the rural enviroment, and these, in turn, are perceived to be the consequence of societal disregard for the rural minority and of the consequent powerlessness of rural citizens[36].

In the U.S. it is expected that generalists, particulary rural generalists, should have the ability to intervene at all levels of the system.

> 'It has been our experience, verified by colleagues in many fields of rural practice, that there are five essential roles that are central to rural practice. They are also appropriate for different systemic levels of a target population, from individual to group to an aggregate of persons (community). These roles are broker, technical expert, consultant, manager of change processes and advocate'[34].

These various roles imply that the social worker should be acquainted with and have some comfort with community work tools, a task for which practitioners should be prepared in training courses.

In Britain theoretical recommendations have also widely supported a pattern of macro involvement by social workers. Grant, for example, has suggested that if rural social workers and community workers were seen 'to be part of a system which embodies public participation at the local level' then their efforts would lead to the formulation of policies which harmonise the contributions of the statutory and voluntary sectors[37].

In reporting a pilot project carried out at the Hereford and Worcester SSD Taylor[38] argued the project corroborated the need for a community orientation in rural service delivery. Taylor spelled out a possible scheme within which this could be carried out. He used the term 'community oriented social worker' to refer 'specifically to a member of an area team within a Social Services Department ... who as well as carrying a caseload also has a wider community brief concerned with the collective needs of the people living in a particular area'[38].

> 'While the employment of a specialist community worker might have its use in certain identifiable problem areas, in the countryside the concept of a community oriented social worker is likely to have more widespread relevance'[38].

In practice, however, at least in 1980, social workers in the SSDs seemed to function narrowly within the scope of traditional casework methodology[39]. Instances where workers were functioning with groups or intervening with communities were very rare. In fact, the rural authorities I visited employed community workers as specialists who functioned quite separately. In Wiltshire, for example, the four community workers in the SSD, whose designation was that of 'Community Development Officers', were functioning primarily as consultant specialists, and although within the Salisbury team the CDO has been successful in establishing groups of volunteers in a variety of ongoing projects and was readily accepted by the social work staff, it was quite apparent that the social work personnel was not eager or able to expand its parameters into community work. In most teams visited, it was clear that whenever community oriented tasks were encountered in daily practice, they were referred to the community work specialists.

The relationship of community work and social work in the rural teams would need a current reassessment in light of the controversial Barclay[29] recommendations. Barclay's proposals for community social work would seem to have particular applicability in rural units. In fact, some of Barclay's critics dubbed the report the 'organisational variant of small is beautiful'[40]. It does seem as if Barclay's alternatives would be most appropriate in small communities where social workers could never, because of size, divorce themselves from all feasible networks of community support, whether existing or in need of creation. It would be unfortunate if Barclay's community orientation, which might be most applicable to teams in remote locations were dismissed because they are inapplicable in all enviroments.

Meadows and Harwood[41] have raised the question of community work specialism v. social work generalism in relation to rural community tasks in the U.K.

> 'If we accept the philosophy that social work is more than meeting the apparent needs of individuals then this raises the question about modes of operation and roles and locations of workers in a rural context. Do we, for example, need solely to widen the brief of social workers to include some involvement in community issues or do we also need community development

workers? Can we continue to practice social work within a departmental frame of reference or do we need to engage with others in a corporate approach. These questions do not apply solely to rural areas but the specific rural context must be a factor in the debate and influence subsequent action'[41].

Perhaps the social work process should start by dismissing the widespread assumption that all community work is revolutionary, or at least confrontative. It has been shown that in the rural areas, locality development tasks play a central or more central role than a social action[33]*.

> 'The basic goal of the social action practitioner is to make fundamental changes in both communities and society. This necessitates shifts in traditional power relationships and decision-making processes in rural communites ... and polarisation of the community as well as organisation of the 'oppressed' to take action against the 'oppressor'

Jacobsen sees these social action tasks as problematic in rural communities unless much 'conscientising' work is done among rural dwellers, a task that statutory workers can seldom seriously undertake. Jacobsen sees locality development as a more applicable and less abrasive model for practioners to use in rural communities.

> 'The model for community change called locality development by Rothman has the practitioner working at the local levels with a broad cross-section of people involved in determining and solving their own problems. In this role the practitioner focuses upon facilitation of the process of community development. The critical elements in this process are a number of small task oriented groups of community residents. The responsibility for the success or failure of the groups and the process rests with the community, not the practitioner'[33].

* Jacobsen bases his analysis on the Rothman model which distinguishes among the goals and methods of the three basic approaches of community work: social action, locality development and planning.

In practice, however, Jacobsen's proposals regarding locality development as the most amenable model for rural community interventions, seems corroborated by U.K. observations where social action is perceived as problematic. Workers are constrained by their agencies and by their accountability to the Social Services Committee from confronting the power structures. Confrontation politics is not seen as the proper realm of officers but as the prerogative of elected officials

'Officers advise, elected representative decide', is very much the accepted guiding principle. Social workers in the SSDs often expressed their discomfort with the possibility of having to confront the authorities that employ them, were they to participate in social action efforts[38]. To encourage a community orientation among social workers - and I am here referring to the enabler and mobiliser roles - considerable reassurance that by-and-large social workers utilise conciliatory roles would have to be given by managers and planners alike.

Finally in the U.K. in 1980, it appeared as if two contradictory forces were operating at the same time. While there was a push toward geographically-contained genericism and generalist practice (i.e. patches), there was also a drive toward efficiency and accountability often perceived at the local authority level as a need to centralise power and decision-making. This centralisation necessarily led away from genericisms and generalism (i.e. avoiding duplication of roles, encouraging the most 'efficient' use of staff within the large teams by permitting workers to have an area of specialism). Specialisation of labour is the distinguishing mark of bureaucratic structures. The more 'efficient' in terms of output or production an organisation wishes to become, the more likely it is to routinise and parcel out its tasks, away from global approaches. SSDs were no exception; thus, the drive for efficiency was a drive away from genericism and even generalism, with its apparently elusive community work dimensions.

A comment in 'Social Work Today' at the height of the controversy over Barclay corroborates this point[27]:

> 'Firstly, our departmental masters prefer us to concentrate on small scale practical and psychological problems; they are

politically uncontentious - budgeting schemes for the poor are fine - attempts to get local authorities and public utilities to acknowledge that impossible fuel bills are in some areas an inevitable consequence of poor planning and building techniques, are not fine.

Secondly, things get uncomfortable at a serious management level when social workers cross department borderlines. It is fine to visit truants and their families at home, as if the causes of school refusal were always to be found there. It is not so easy to get backing for perfectly sensible projects, involving both social workers and teachers which aim to look inside the schools for some of the causes of school absence and educational disadvantage'.

In the eyes of the managers, individual problems have always seemed to be more finite, safer, amenable to intervention and accountability. Those tendencies towards an 'output' model of accountability are distressing to all generalists but particularly rural generalists who spend a great deal of time on tasks that do not render immediate client output (e.g. driving; becoming 'known' and 'visible'). Measuring the efficiency of generalist workers by traditional indices also worries rural managers in the U.S. who function under 'field' constrictions. For example, it is easier to demonstrate 'efficiency' in casework intervention in child welfare than it is to justify why a child welfare worker spent a whole day on a case while working as a generalist, although he/she may have helped the child, the parents and grandparents and set up a number of community networks for future use.

'Traditional cost-benefit studies usually employ monetary measurements in assessing systems. Social services workers are well aware of the implicit hazards of borrowing such methods... If we are to borrow profitably techniques which might be utilised in our attempts to more equitably distribute rural social services, we must not forget that our objectives ... cannot always be measured in economic terms'[42].

Perhaps the way to proceed, as Culyer[43] and Herrick[42] have argued, is through cost-benefit and cost-effectiveness methods which would assess the costs not just of accessibility but of inaccessibility to selected rural social services.

Conclusion

It appears as if generalist practice as an approach that encompasses micro and macro level interventions continues to be quite appropriate for the rural areas. The nature of the relationship between the social worker and the small community precludes the artificial separation of individuals from their community milieu, even when the practice is approached from a field-specialist perspective (see, for example the model presented by Deaton and Morgan[44] when co-ordinating community resources around child protective services). In the U.K. both the literature on rural patches[28] and the recommendations of Barclay[29] seem to highlight the need for a rural generalist who will focus on both the individual and the community.

On the other hand, genericism, that is practice across fields, seems to be a point of debate. In the U.K. recent reports from some of the teams in the Scottish Highlands seem to attest to the continued controversy. For example the Highland Region social work director argues:

> 'We've identified that the problem which staff labour under is having to have a high level of skill in a wide variety of fields... Therefore time and energy are wasted seeking consultation and, since management is not willing to risk junior members of staff making decisions which are drastically wrong, if you are not careful you tend to get a sort of creeping bureaucratisation'[45].

The problem is very real. In the U.S., because the social services are still organised by fields, the dilemma is not as acute and seems to have been resolved in favour of a generalist metholodogy with a degree of specialisation by field, more or less accentuated, depending on the remoteness of the area, the number of service providers available, and the extent to which agencies work cooperatively. In the U.S., the rural field seems to be evolving into a field where specialist-generalists function, albeit sometimes less than comfortably. In the U.K., a movement towards specialisation could be seen as a movement away from 'patches', a problematic situation for those who favour decentralisation and locality specific practice. Perhaps the solution to the specialist/ generalist controversy is one of degree. The degree of specialisation of workers within the basic generic framework is a matter to be decided more by common sense than by prescription. For, again as the recent report from the Highland's Director states[45]:

> 'You cannot sensibly serve the remote areas with a team of specialist social workers - it just does not make sense. You must be able to call on specialist skills beyond the generic skill just as local GPs call on a consultant skill. But it is entirely feasible to operate the Cromarty Firth area on specialist lines, and that is something that is beginning to be discussed at all levels within the department'.

LOCALITY-SPECIFIC OR LOCALISM IN RURAL SERVICE DELIVERY

Because the term localism like community has been used to denote quite different and even opposing approaches, it is important to clarify how its meaning has evolved from a fairly contained and non-controversial way of describing what was needed in rural service delivery, to a politically loaded term that could presumably entail the demise of social work as we know today. Controversies created by the uses and misuses of the concept of localism in social work seem to be common not only in the U.S. but also in the U.K. A recent comment by Sheldon[27] summarises this problem well:

> 'It is not surprising that community-based approaches to social work evoke, albeit for different reasons, the approval of radicals and conservatives alike since the idea of community is both intangible and paradoxical. It is intangible because it has not yet been satisfactorily defined in the setting of an industrial society, and paradoxical because historically it has inspired some of the most paternalistic philosophies of social welfare and some of the most libertarian ones'.

In the U.S., what was in the early days of the rural movement meant by locality-specific social work was a methodological approach. Just as social workers had to be able to individualise services for particular clients, they had to be able to make services locality-specific, that is relevant to particular regions or locales. As early as 1936, U.S. rural social workers were warned that 'having a knowledge of rural life in one section of the country' does not qualify a worker to undertake social service in any rural area; with all their variation, cities are standardised in comparison with the rural areas[46]. As time went on and social workers developed more assertive political stances and as their relationships with local communities were strengthened, strong connections between social work to grass-roots organising began to emerge. Grass-roots groups identified indigenous or locality-specific issues, developed goals and searched for solutions to local problems[47]. Efforts to identify locality-specific issues are viewed as part of the traditional methodology of social work which advises to 'start where the client is' and 'to proceed with the least intrusive solutions or interventions' first.

Unfortunately, the burden of identifying issues, values and norms unique to particular localities, has often rested with individual workers who may or may not have the ability to identify similarities and dissimilarites among co-existing cultural groups. In the U.S. the recent emphasis placed on training students who are sensitive to the needs of racial or ethnic minorities has secondarily helped develop a core of social workers who are responsive to local idiosyncratic needs. The literature in the U.S. and Canada has begun to show this tailoring to rural uniqueness[48][49][50]. The incorporation of locality-specific or locality relevant content seems to be a fairly non-controversial aspect of localism in both the U.S. and the U.K. In Scotland, for example, where local issues have always been attended to with great concern, a heightened awareness of locality-specific practice permeates current rural social work discussion[45]. In Wales, issues of language and sensitivity to very local concerns among the elderly are often discussed in the literature. And in England, advocates of patches, for example, stress regional idiosyncracies and uniqueness[28].

A second meaning of localism in the U.S. emerged when practitioners became concerned about the impediments that centralised administration in distant cities (whether Washington, D.C. or state capitals) represented for service delivery in the rural and remote regions of the nation. Advocates of localism, meaning decentralisation in the administration of services, received much support from rural liberals[51], and albeit for differt reasons, from conservatives and country-life romantics[52] who had always dreamed of an idyllic scenario of direct democracy in the local areas. Both in the U.K. and the U.S. social workers bemoan the tendency of organisations to centralise decision-making away from the people affected, which is characteristic of bureaucratic systems. Patch proponents have made decentralisation one of their central beliefs [53].

Centralisation in social service decision-making is fairly ingrained in the U.S. While under the current conservative administration the federal government has turned many functions to the states, state bureaucracies are still massive and often just as remote from counties, small towns and villages.

Centralisation is also very pronounced in the formulation of policies. 'By and large social services depamtents are fairly highly centralised agencies whose functions are ill understood by the community at large'[54]. The outcome of legislation through the years has been that SSDs provide an array of very similar functions, which vary little from region to region or from one locality to another. This assumption, however, has been repeatedly questioned by proponents of 'patches'[28]. While 'patches' might not modify the basic service package, they clearly modify its delivery. Of course, centralistic assumptions were also challenged in the context of the commmunity-based model proposed by the Barclay Committee[29]. The heated debate of the Barclay proposals centred around basic questions such as could social workers be realistically expected to provide statutory services and nurture the natural networks of communities?

The current perception in the U.S. is that social workers should try to do both, provide mandated services and work with the small community in a developmental role[33][55], although it must be recognised that the literature on this matter is often more prescriptive than descriptive. It must also be recognised that social workers in the voluntary sector are less constrained by statutory demands from acting as local community advocates. Voluntary boards are more accessible and vulnerable, thus more responsive to worker and client demands.

In 1980, the desire of many rural practitioners in the U.K. was to move towards the introduction of 'decentralised' thinking into the problem solving paradigm of the sparsely populated or rural areas. For example, Varwell[7] formulated a number of recommendations for the Highland Regional Council in Scotland. His suggestions were based on the results of a study tour in the sparsely populated areas of Norway, Iceland and the Faroe Islands and amounted to recommending a locality based and indigenous oriented practice to the rural authorities of the sparsely populated regions of Scotland. Varwell's recommendations were also a strong call for support in developing a local consciousness as manifested by the use of the indigenous language[7]. Varwell in fact suggested that the health of the language was directly related to the health of the small community. A fair number of Welsh practitioners concurred with Varwell on this matter.

A series of research projects based in rural areas were designed to investigate the most appropriate ways of delivering services to the rural locale and are likely to establish and test out indigenous responses to local needs. For example, the Gwynedd Social Services Department in cooperation with the Citizen's Advice Bureau, has established a mobile van to travel in rural areas. Schemes like these vans, supplemented by static bureaus located in the larger towns, would 'not simply act as a referral points for persons in need of personal social services' but have a very positive preventative role insofar as more direct diffusion of information to rural dwellers is likely to enhance the community's ability to act and make decisions independently of urban service centres [54].

A third meaning of localism in the U.S. emerged with the Reagan administration. In this latter sense, the localism theme became tied up with curtailing of federal funds allocated to the social services. Reagan's proposals assumed that in local communities, the informal and voluntary systems would pick up on services that might no longer be provided through federal dollars. It is in this sense, that localism became a very controversial and downright ideological corollary.

Critiques of localism and 'patches' have been levied by U.K. social workers[56], and some of the worries about the proposals of conservative governments seem to be similar in the U.S. and U.K. Critics of the Barclay Report, for example, have remarked:

> 'The most localised system of social service in the history of British social policy was the Poor Law. Its relieving and guardians all served localities that were sufficiently small to be intimately known. It was just this distinctive quality of parochial social service that added a uniquely hurtful dimension to the experience of stigma among recipients of poor relief'[57].

It is important to distinguish between locality-relevant delivery of social services and locally-based funding for social work. The latter, of course, would bring us back to the era of only voluntary or informal services for the rural areas, an event that few rural workers envisage. In the U.S. rural social work has had a long tradition of shared responsibility by the informal, the voluntary and the public sectors [58]. It must be remembered, however, that much funding for the voluntary sector comes from government, through the system of purchase of care. Government is often involved in encouraging informal networks; thus, diminished public commitment to the social services would affect the total picture of care in the rural areas.

While it is more appropriate for social workers to recognise the merits of local, informal care givers, there are certain services that will never be informally provided. Local care givers, for example, often become agents of prevention in child neglect cases, supporting overwhelmed parents or relieving care-takers in temporary distress, but even ministers are reluctant to intervene in cases of extreme abuse or with parents who have completely shut-out communication with the community. As for the role of supporting natural care-givers in rural communities, social workers must carry out this task if they are to supplement rather than supplant existing services. In the U.S. in recent years, a contentious and litigious model of personal rights and privacy has emerged which makes it very hard and sometimes impossible to maintain the helpful involvement of significant others. Confidentiality and individual rights have to be reassessed if they are to be useful principles in rural community service[13].

In summary, under the label of rural localism, social workers have addressed at least three dimensions of local community participation:

1. identifying local issues and needs that are unique to particular areas;
2. identifying loci of decision-making that are closer to the communities being served;
and
3. identifying support networks and other local strengths which, if appropriately nurtured, might be reliable in one area, but unreliable in another.

It is important for managers and service providers to be clear about which dimension is being addressed at any given time.

SUMMARY AND CONCLUSIONS

When in 1980, during the field study in the U.K. I visited selected SSDs in England, Scotland and Wales and attempted to assess whether the issues that concerned rural social workers in the U.S. transcended national barriers, I was struck by the similarity of many practice problems. This paper has focused on two tenets of rural practice that still represent common concerns of practitioners and managers in the U.S. and U.K. in 1984.

Generic and generalist practice are still key concerns of rural workers in the two nations. What seems to have happened is that as conservative governments moved in the direction of cutting the cost of social work services (safety nets vs. welfare state provisions), rural social work was forced to analyse genericism and generalist practice from a pragmatic rather than ideological perspective. Pragmatism is not necessarily an unhealthy approach to issue analysis. Rural social workers are still committed to generic and generalist practice, but issues of cost and accountability are now more at the forefront of decision-making than issues of philosophy. Successful genericism and generalism are a question of fit. When does it make sense to approach practice from a generic or crossfield perspective? When does it not? When is it imperative for social workers to intervene in individual and community systems simultaneously? When can such interventions be best carried out by community work specialists? Just as casework intervention alone can put blinders on the way in which workers perceive social phenomena, so a forced or artificial community thrust can result in inappropriate interventions. What rural areas must have are workers who are capable of and feel comfortable intervening at various levels of the system. Determining when to reach out to the community for care and when not to rely on it is a matter of judgement rather than prescription.

In addition rural social workers have become more concerned with personal burn-out and survival. It is not recognised that the demands of generic and generalist practice are great and that not all individuals working in rural areas might be equipped to handle them. The compromise position of the 'specialist-generalist' is a sensible one as long as the region is not too remote and as long as workers look at the clients' interests rather than their own convenience in deciding who should be involved in any one case. Keeping this in mind, the 'specialist-generalist' might not be an inappropriate worker model for many rural teams in the U.K. Within the framework of a generic team, workers could enjoy a degree of specialisation by field while still remaining capable of intervening at 'all levels of the system' (individuals and communities).

Regarding the relationship of social work to the community, rural workers have continued to discuss and highlight the importance of informal and voluntary service schemes of social care in rural areas. They have continued to stress the importance of their community role as mobilisers, enablers and empowerers of rural dwellers. The problem for rural social work seems to be preventing conservative governments from misinterpreting the extent to which community action (whether natural or formalised) can supplant the formal system and from over using a valid and meritorious reliance on natural helpers to justify constricting political agendas. Social workers are never justified in usurping the role of the natural or voluntary system, but it must be remembered that those systems are incapable of dealing with many problems and there are times when the impersonal bureaucracy can best perform the helping task.

On the issue of providing services which are locality specific, no one questions the need to tailor responses to particular areas or populations or the advisability of debureaucratising and making services easily accessible. From the recent debate over localism, however, comes the warning that not all problems can be solved locally or by intimate networks; locally based solutions in the personal social services are appropriate options in many cases but not in all.

In summary, what current rural social work efforts have done is help social work in general focus on community oriented practice principles which might be more overtly applicable to the rural and remote areas but are not inapplicable elsewhere.

'Locality-specific' practice principles warn against transplanting solutions from one setting to another. While solid practice principles need never be exclusively urban or exclusively rural, no principle, urban or rural, should ever be generalised without appropriate scrutiny of local conditions and trial testing.

References

1. Newby, H., Bell, C., Rose, D. & Saunders, P. Property, Paternalism and Power. Class and Control in Rural England. The University of Wisconsin Press, Madison, 1978.
2. Hechter, M. Internal Colonialism. The Celtic Fringe in British National Development 1536-1966. University of California Press, Berkeley, 1975.
3. Essen, J. & Wedge, P. Continuities in Childhood Disadvantage. DHSS Studies in Deprivation and Disadvantage 6, Heinemann Educational Books, London 1982.
4. Broady, M. Marginal Regions: Essays on Social Planning. Bedford Square Press, London, 1973.
5. Broady, M. 'The Drumbuie Inquiry: David and Goliath in Scottish Rural Development' Community Development Journal. Vol 10 (April), 1975.

6. Carter, I. 'The Highlands of Scotland As An Underdeveloped Region' in de Kadt, E. & Williams, G. (Eds.) Sociology and Development. Tavistock, London, 1974.
7. Varwell, A. Social Work Service and the Contribution of Community Development in a Sparsely Populated Area. Report of Council of Europe Fellowship Study Tour to Norway, Iceland and the Faroe Islands, 1978.
8. Caudill, H.M. Night comes to the Cumberlands : Biography of a Depressed Area. Little, Brown, Boston 1963.
9. Strasser, J. 'The Land is no Escape' in Rodefield, R.D., Jan, F., Voth, D., Fujimoto, I. & Converse, J. (Eds.) Change in Rural America. Causes, Consequences and Alternatives. The C.V. Mosby Co., St. Louis 1978.
10. Abramson, J.A. 'Types of Rural Communities' in Shera, W. (Ed.) Rural Social Work Forum Conference Proceedings. 1979, 11-64.
11. Jordan, D. 'Kansas Out-Migration. Focus on Centralia' in Rodefield, R.D., Jan, F., Voth, D., Fujimoto, I. & Converse, J., (Eds.) Change in Rural America. Causes, Consequences and Alternatives. The C.V. Mosby Co., St. Louis, 1978.
12. Fenby, B.L. 'Social Work in a Rural Setting' Social Work. Vol. 23, No.2 (March) 1978, 162-163.
13. Moore-Kirkland, J. & Irey, K.V. 'A Reappraisal of Confidentiality' Social Work. Vol. 26, No.4 (July) 1981, 319-322.
14. Cooper, M. 'Interweaving Social Work and the Community' in Hadley, R. & McGrath, M. Going Local. Neighbourhood Social Service. N.C.V.O. Bedford Square Press, London, 1980, 29-40.
15. Sheridan, P. 'Developing a Patch System in the Inner City' in Hadley, R. & McGrath, M. Going Local. Neighbourhood Social Service. N.C.V.O. Bedford Square Press, London, 1980, 55-62.
16. Hey, A. 'Not by Patch Alone' Appendix C., in Martinez-Brawley, E.E. Rural Social and Community Work in the U.S. and Britain. Praegar, N.Y. 1982, 240-246.
17. Magill, R.S. & Clark, T.N. 'Community Power and Decision Making: Recent Research and Its Policy Implications' Social Service Review. Vol. 49, No.1 (March) 1975,33-45.
18. Saunders, P., Newby, H., Bell, C. & Rose, D. 'Rural Community and Rural Community Power' in Newby, H. (Ed.) International Perspectives in Rural Sociology. John Wiley and Sons, N.Y. 1978, Chapter 3, 55-85.

19. Times-Union. 'The Flight to the Country. Rural Areas, Small Towns Grow Faster than Urban Areas' Rochester, N.Y., March 3, 1981, p.5A.
20. Findlay, S.B. 'Values in Conflict - The Rural Practice Iceberg' in Richard, L.J. & St. Amand, N. (Eds.) Values in Conflict. University of Moncton, Memramcook, New Brunswick, 1980, 96-115.
21. Martinez-Brawley, E.E. 'Rural Social Work Tenets in the United States and Latin America: A Cross-Cultural Comparison' Community Development Journal. 15 (October) 1980, 167-178.
22. Martinez-Brawley, E.E. Rural Social and Community Work in the U.S. and Britain. Praeger, N.Y., 1982.
23. Shera, W. (Ed.) Rural Social Work Forum Conference Proceedings. Victoria, British Columbia, 1979.
24. Buxton, E.B. 'Delivering Social Services in Rural Areas' in Ginsberg, L. (Ed.) Social Work in Rural Communities. A Book of Readings. Council on Social Work Education, New York, 1976, 29-38
25. Mermelstein, J & Sundet, P. 'Social Work Education for Rural Program Development' in Ginsberg, L. (Ed.) Social Work in Rural Communities. A Book of Readings. Council on Social Work Education, New York, 1976, 13-27
26. Levin, L. (Ed.) Educating Social Workers for Practice in Rural Settings: Perspectives and Programs. Southern Regional Educational Board, Atlanta, 1974.
27. Sheldon, B. 'A Romantic Illusion' Social Work Today. Vol. 13, No. 46, (October 8) 1982, 10-12.
28. Hadley, R. & McGrath, M. Going Local. Neighbourhood Social Services. N.C.V.O. Bedford Square Press, London, 1980.
29. Barclay, P.M. Chairman, Social Workers Their Role and Tasks. The Report of a Working Party. National Institue of Social Work, Bedford Square Press, London 1982.
30. Daley, J.M. Price, C.P. & Price, R.P. 'A Rural Practice Model: Evaluation' in Davenport, J., Davenport, J.A. & Wiebler, J.R. (Eds.) Social Work in Rural Areas: Issues and Opportunities. University of Wyoming, Laramie, 1980, 181-185.
31. Anderson, J.D. 'Generic and Generalsit Practice and the BSW Curriculum' Journal of Education for Social Work. Vol. 18, No.3 (Fall) 1982, 37-45.
32. Omer, S. 'Rural Practice Models: Community Development' in Green, R.K. and Webster, S.A. (Eds.) Social Work in Rural

Areas: Preparation and Practice. University of Tennessee, School of Social Work, Knoxville, 1977, 107-136.

33. Jacobsen, M.G. 'Rural Communities and Community Development' in Johnson, W.H. (Ed.) Rural Human Services. A Book of Readings. Peacock Publishers, Itasca, Ill., 1980, 196-202.

34. Mermelstein, J. & Sundet, P. 'Worker Aceptance and Credibility in the Rural Enviroment' in Johnson, W. (Ed.) Rural Human Services. A Book of Readings. Peacock Publishers, Itasca, Ill., 1980, 174-178.

35. Couch, D., Dutton, E., Gurss, A. & Serpan, T. 'A Specialist-Generalist Model of Social Work Practice for Contemporary Rural America' In Green, R.K. & Webster, S.R. (Eds.) Social Work in Rural Areas: Preparation and Practice. University of Tennessee School of Social Work, Knoxville, 1977, 95-106.

36. Wellstone, P. How the Rural Poor Got Power. Narrative of a Grass-Roots Organiser. University of Massachusetts Press, Amherst, 1978.

37. Grant, G. 'Approaches to Social Welfare Delivery in Rural Areas' Paper delivered at the European Centre for Social Welfare Training and Research on Social Welfare Delivery in the Rural Areas. Sesimbra, Portugal, November 12-16 1979, (mimeo).

38. Taylor, H. An Evaluation of the Effectiveness of Social Services Provisions in a Rural Area. University of Birmingham, Department of Social Administration, Social Services Unit, in collaboration with the Social Services Department, County Council of Hereford and Worcester, 1976.

39. Stevenson, O. & Parsloe, P. Social Service Teams: The Practitioner's View. HMSO, DHSS, London 1978.

40. Welch, I. 'Love thy Neighbourhood' Social Work Today. Vol. 13, No.46, (October 8) 1982, 7-9.

41. Meadows, A. & Harwood, F. 'Changing Rural Communities; Social Work Today. Vol. 10 (September 4) 1978, 27-28.

42. Herrick, J. 'Social Service Accessibility: Is Location Relevant?' In Davenport, J. Davenport, J.A. & Wiebler, J.R. (Eds.) Social Work in Rural Areas: Issues and Opportunities. University of Wyoming, Laramie, 1980, 186-193.

43. Culyer, A.J. The Economics of Social Policy. Martin Robertson, London, 1973.

44. Deaton, B. & Morgan, D. 'Tough Times: Community Coordination and Development in Child Protective Services in a Rural Area' in Jacobsen, M.G. (Ed.) Nourishing People and Communities

Through the Lean Years. University of Iowa, 1982, 120-126.
45. Social Work Today. 'Behind the Scenery', reported by Rob Edwards, Vol.14 No.27, (March 15) 1983, 10-11.
46. Gerson, S. & Gerson, J. 'The Social Worker in the Rural Community' in Martinez-Brawley, E.E. (Ed.) Pioneer Efforts in Rural Social Welfare. First Hand Views Since 1908. Pennsylvania State University Press, 1980, 380-387.
47. Whitaker, W.H. 'Making Waves in A Sea of Peanut Butter: Implications for Social Work Practice in Sparsely Populated, Conservative Areas' in Davenport, J., Davenport, J.A. & Wiebler, J.R. (Eds.) Social Work in Rural Areas: Issues and Opportunities. University of Wyoming, Laramie, 1980, 194-204.
48. Clemmons Morris, L. (Ed.) Dignity, Diversity and Opportunity in Changing Rural Areas. The University of South Carolina, Columbia, 1982.
49. Clarke, K. 'Professional Social Work Values as Experienced by a Student: Social Work in the Northwest River' in Richard, L.J. & St. Amand, N. (Eds.) Values in Conflict. University of Moncton, Memramcook , New Brunswick, 1980, 116-136.
50. Duncombe, P. 'Considerations in the Cross-Cultural Delivery of Social Services to Native Americans' in Davenport, J., Davenport, J.A. & Wiebler, J.R. (Eds.) Social Work in Rural Areas: Issues and Opportunities. University of Wyoming, Laramie, 1980, 137-151.
51. Hightower, J. 'Run at Them' Ruralamerica. 5, No.9, (Dec./Jan.) 1980, p.6.
52. Martinez-Brawley, E.E. 'Localism: New Definitions Disturb Rural Social Workers' NASW News. Vol.26, No.6 (June) 1981, P.7.
53. Jones, G. 'South Hereford. Nature Makes No Leaps' in Hadley, R. & McGrath, M. Going Local. Neighbourhood Services. N.C.V.O. Bedford Square Press, London, 1980, 16-28.
54. Grant, G. 'The Provision of Social Services in Rural Areas' in Williams, G. (Ed.) Social and Cultural Change in Contemporary Wales. Routledge & Kegan Paul, London, 1978, 61-75.
55. Bedics, B.C. & Doelker, R. 'Mobilising Informal Resources in Rural Communities' Human Services in the Rural Enviroment. Vol.8, No. 1, 1983, 18-23.
56. Community Care. 'The Politics of Patch' March 4th 1982, 12-13.
57. Pinker, R.A. 'An Alternative View' Appendix B, Barclay, P.M. (Chairman) Social Workers: Their Role and Tasks. The Report of the Working Party, National Institute for Social Work, Bedford

Square Press, London, 1982.
58. Johnson, L.C. 'Human Service Delivery Patterns in Nonmetropolitan Communities' in Johnson, W. (Ed.) Rural Human Services. A Book of Readings. Peacock Publishers, Itasca, Ill., 1980, 65-74.

RESIDENTIAL AND DAY SERVICES - CHANGE IN A CHANGING CONTEXT

Philip Seed

In this paper I propose to examine current changes in residential and day care against the background of wider societal changes which are visible in comparing urban and rural contexts. Some of these changes are sudden. For example[1]:

> 'I well remember the inn yard at Exeter where we stabled our pony in a long row of farmers' dog carts ... for it was market day, how not more than four years later the carts had disappeared; their place was taken by a row of snub nosed Morris and Ford cars'.

Although sometimes sudden in their effects, the kinds of changes affecting rural and urban settings and living patterns are mostly long-standing and persistent. They include rural depopulation, centralisation of major consumer and social services, especially education and health services, the impact of industrial development (e.g. oil) and suburbanisation of some rural areas. The phenomenon of poor ghetto areas in inner cities is likewise not new, though its effects may be newly and dramatically felt in specific situations.

Residential and day care is also characterised by continuous change which, locally, can have sudden and dramatic consequences. For example, the 1978 Directory of Residential Facilities in Scotland[2] lists Quarrier's Homes, Bridge of Weir, in Strathclyde as catering for 480 children in small cottage units. The 1984 Directory relocates it under 'Special Care' and shows it offering 190 places. The consequences, ramifications and causes of a change like this are enormous for staff, children, other agencies and the community[3]. They have to be set in the context of changes in urban and rural settings. In each case we can ask: What is new? What has changed? What remains? In the case of Quarrier's, the social landscape has changed as dramatically as the physical landscape appeared to change when the cars replaced the dog carts in Exeter's market place many years ago.

This article seeks to address the underlying question of the inter-relationship of changes in urban and rural contexts and changes in residential and day care services. It must be said at the outset that this is a question which no particular piece of research has, as far as I know, specifically tackled. Perhaps the most this article can do is to raise a number of questions on the basis of slender connections which local or regional studies point to, and to set these in the context of argument deduced from wider research relating both to community and societal change, and to residential and day care.

GENERAL CHANGES IN RESIDENTIAL AND DAY CARE

It may be helpful to begin by summarising current changes in residential and day care in Britain. It is easier, of course, to identify changes in policy intentions, and changing perceptions of residential and day care tasks, than to say precisely what these mean in practice. The following list applies generally to residential and day care as a whole. Changes in policies and practice for particular client groups have been discussed in earlier issues of RESEARCH HIGHLIGHTS dealing with the elderly[4], children[5], the handicapped[6], and offenders[7]. A useful recent discussion of changes in child care policies is the Strathclyde Regional Council's Report 'Home or Away'[8].

1. More attention is being given to the idea of locality. This has various aspects:

(a) Growing use of day care facilities[9]. This raises the issue of daily access.

(b) Growing links between residential and day care. This highlights the question of siting.

(c) In general, the expectation that both residential and day care establishments will draw on local community resources, and serve local community needs. This emphasises the question of context.

2. Some kinds of once-valued specialist provisions are now being questioned. On the one hand there is an integration of client categories for some services e.g. some facilities for the mentally and physically handicapped. On the other hand, some special groups are attracting more attention as some client categories are receiving separate provision: e.g. alcoholics, battered wives. The alternation of ideas favouring first specialist and then non-specialist provision in residential and day care has a long history [10]. There tends to be a pendulum kind of movement though at the moment, it must be said, pendulums are moving in different directions in different fields, which makes the problem of planning facilities complex.

3. Some kinds of establishments are being closed while others, threatened with closure, are adapting to new circumstances where different kinds of residential and day care are required. Other establishments are still being built. The complex set of factors producing these changes includes the following:

(a) Some large, traditional institutions in city centres are closing or adapting, because they are no longer considered appropriate forms of provision. Lodging houses are an example[2].

(b) More centralised and separate systems of provision are out of step with the trend towards locality based services. These include, for example, the List D system in Scotland[11]. (Some List D schools are moving to provide day care, for which they may not be ideally sited, though, paradoxically, it is where many of them began as day industrial schools over 130 years ago[10].)

(c) It is intended that there should be a changing balance of care from hospital-based to community-based residential and day care services. At the same time, the community-based provisions are themselves under scrutiny (e.g. hostels, so-called half-way houses, and adult training centres).

(d) Though not a new idea, there is a growing interest in providing 'respite care'.

(e) There is an intention to reduce the amount of residential provision for some groups in favour of fostering or adoption. The extent to which this is occurring varies from area to area.

(f) For the residential and day services which are being developed there are higher expectations of professional staffing and demands for higher staff-client ratios.

(g) At the same time there is concern about escalating costs.

4. There is growing recognition of private care establishments, especially for the elderly and also for disturbed children[12].

5. There is an increasing interest in forms of special housing as a social service for groups who might otherwise be in residential hospital or other caring establishments.

The interrelationship of these changes in residential and day care and wider societal change will be discussed around three themes. The first is the meaning of locality and its implications. The second is the tension between planning and responding in social service provision. The third is the relationship (or apparent lack of relationship) between social work policies and economic aspects of community development. The argument is that these themes raise issues which, while not exclusive to rural or to urban areas, are nevertheless highlighted in rural, and especially remote, settings and this will be shown by some examples of research findings.

LOCALITY

Locality raises key issues for residential and day care services in rural areas. Because these services require more capital provision than fieldwork services, financial factors more readily play a part in determining how localised provision can be. For example, in determining how large an establishment should be, regard is paid during the planning process to such factors as the optimum size in terms of staffing and economic costs. Even if minimum regard is paid to such factors, and rural residential services are developed on the basis of such very small multi-purpose units as can be found, for example, in parts of the Highlands and Western Isles[13], this still would not make it possible to have a separate facility in every village. Travel is a prerequisite for those in residential care to be able to maintain contact with relations and the ability to travel daily is a prerequisite for day care unless residential provision associated with day care is also provided (which could be thought of as a bit of a contradiction).

An example of this in 'normal' education provision is the use of hostels in some rural areas of Scotland to enable pupils to attend secondary schools[12]. Without their use, together with education lodgings, the catchment areas of secondary schools could not possibly be so large. In some cases, the same kind of consideration has led to the development of hostels alongside adult training centres for the mentally handicapped.

Ideally, the development of locality-based services in rural areas would imply not only smaller, geographically dispersed residential and day care facilities but also more localised control. This is especially true where cultural differences between areas add to the meanings ascribed to more distant decision-making locations[13]. Yet it must be said that the tendency within social work and social service agencies still often tends to be towards more centralised control[14].

THE TENSION BETWEEN PLANNING AND RESPONDING IN SOCIAL SERVICE PROVISION

New residential and day care establishments, especially when they are purpose-built (which local authorities tend to prefer where finance allows) are developed from plans which are (a) long-term and often part of larger long-term plans (b) often conceived a long time before they become operational (c) entail interdepartmental collaboration at different levels (e.g. collaboration between architects, personnel and administration and finance departments, as well as with social workers). These complexities sometimes make it difficult to adjust to changing perceptions of need, while the planning or building is still in progress.

A useful framework for discussing these problems in rural areas is suggested by Shaw and Stockford[15]. They distinguish between the planning process and 'responsive services'. This raises the question of how social work, as a responsive service, can operate in the kinds of rural areas where needs are not easily expressed. In our Highlands and Western Isles study[16][17] we discussed expressed and unexpressed needs in terms of looking at referral networks. These had very different features in urban and in remote rural areas. In urban areas the networks led through other existing services. In remote areas where these other services were thin on the ground, or indeed non-existent, referrals of people with a handicap led through a sometimes complex and confusing maze of informal contacts.

Shaw and Stockford found that 80% of referrals to social service departments in England and Wales are via an agency or person other than the client. They comment that:

> 'If, for example, a doctor in a rural practice knows that a meals on wheels service does not exist, it is unlikely he will consider a referral to be of much value'[15].

The availability of services generates their use and also generates demand for related services. In this respect, residential and day care services, especially in today's context of more emphasis on locality, contact with families, and community care generally, operate only in relation to field and domiciliary services and resources. If these are lacking or undeveloped, the expressed need and therefore the response to that need, will also be undeveloped. This, in turn, will inhibit efforts that are being made at more central planning levels to build response into the planning processes. Thus a new residential or day facility can appear to be isolated or out of step from the existing pattern of provision.

Our research in the Highlands suggested that some areas are so remote from the places where needs are, in administrative terms, perceived, counted and incorporated into the planning process, that a kind of fiction arises about what services do exist, and their relevance to faraway places[16][17]. This arises because, in administrative terms, a facility serves a given area up to the place where it meets the boundary of the area served by the next nearest 'adjacent' facility - however large in practical terms the gap between the two centres is. In other words, if it is an authority's policy to provide a 'comprehensive' service for its whole territory, no piece of territory is, by definition, not served. Unmet needs in this situation remain invisible, until the clients or their families themselves find a way, in very difficult circumstances, to articulate demands. Our research suggested that what tends to happen in practice is that:

(1) efforts are made to manage without services either by adapting services intended for other purposes or by using informal helping networks, or

(2) when a situation breaks down because the alternatives to formal services are insufficient, a more drastic solution has to be found through long-term residential (including hospital) care.

The needs which are most exposed in rural areas as being unmet when a thorough search is undertaken, tend to be in terms of the 'intermediate' solutions - including day care, respite care, local half-way houses and so on.

SOCIAL WORK POLICY AND ECONOMIC ASPECTS OF COMMUNITY DEVELOPMENT

Residential and day care services are employers of people - a fact which, in a rural area, is visibly important to the social and economic well-being of the local community. Thus, for example, when the centralisation of hospital services leads to the closure of some local hospitals, this can be seen to have a demoralising effect on the locality in reducing employment opportunities. On the other hand, the opening of a new facility in a rural area can be welcomed in terms of the employment opportunities it provides, because even small numbers count. This was recognised, for example, when a new independent school for children with special needs and later an associated half-way house, attracted financial assistance in the form of grants and loans from the Highlands and Islands Development Board[18]. This economic factor can, indeed, help to offset fears a local community will have about new facilities opening - fears that residents will upset the lives of the local inhabitants.

Very little has been written in Britain about the relationship between social work policy and the economic aspects of community development. Exceptions are Walton[19] and Jones[20], who are also unusual in taking a world perspective and relating this to social work 'on the ground'. Walton discusses these things in the context of deteriorating services which, writing in 1980, he predicted would be a consequence of social and economic policies that might be pursued, and which, in fact, have been pursued. He calls for a world perspective in the kind of language consistent with the Brandt Reports:

> 'The United Kingdom social worker has to adopt a three-way perspective: helping to achieve internal social change; doing this in a way which takes into account the economic and social needs of less developed countries; and promoting forms of social work and social services in Third World countries which are adapted to their economic, social and cultural needs'.

Such a view is a long way from the local view which is likely to be the prevailing perspective in reality. Yet it is in rural areas that the world is often most visibly brought to one's own doorstep - consider the dramatic developments at Invergordon, for example[21], or the situation in a place like Peterhead - where we do have the advantage of a local research study which takes account of social as well as economic issues[22]. Moore suggests that Peterhead illustrates some of the difficulties in distinguishing developed and under-developed areas of the world for, in being at the end of the line from where vital economic and social policy decisions are taken, it is in some ways characteristic of an under-developed region. Even in terms of local decision-making, Peterhead is poorly placed. For example, across countryside largely bereft of public transport, the divisional education office is located nearly 55 miles away in Keith, while the main divisional social work office is 34 miles away in Banff.

Jones turns the comparison between developed and under-developed areas on its head by suggesting we can learn from the failures that third-world countries have experienced[20]:

> 'We have to retrace our steps a lot further than most countries of the third world. We may ... see in ourselves as in a glass darkly much more that it might nevertheless be worthwhile looking at ... we may come to understand better some shortcomings in our approaches to social problems and policies.

He suggests this implies investing more in new kinds of delivery of social services in rural areas which are appropriate to the needs of the locality and which help to redress the imbalance between investment in urban and rural areas.

EXAMPLES

The following examples are intended to illustrate the application of these three themes to residential and day care in rural areas. The examples comprise case studies of day centres in rural areas, the use of services for the elderly, a case study of the key village idea, and a consideration of the role of different social network patterns in assessing differential prevalence rates for children in care in different local authority areas.

Transport to Rural Day Centres

The unremitting withdrawal of public rail and bus transport from rural (and even some urban) areas particularly affects people with a handicap - and especially those with a mental handicap. Firstly, they are likely to be unable to drive a car and, secondly, others in their families who might otherwise drive for them are less likely, as a whole, than the general population, to own their own cars[16], so their reliance on public transport or special transport is very great.

Normalisation policies will favour the use of public, rather than special, transport which may also be favoured on economic grounds. Yet how can this apply when public transport is lacking? The answer is that it cannot, as an evaluation of the adult training centre in Stowmarket recently showed[23]:

> 'Another manifestation of independence is the increase in the number of trainees who make their own way to the centre; fifteen (out of sixty) trainees are no longer dependent on departmental transport and more could be so if public transport was available from outlying rural areas'.

The absence of public rural transport in this case also means greater costs for the special transport provided by the department. We tend to talk about normalisation in terms of special groups using public transport, but less consideration is given to the idea of opening up to the public transport which belongs to a department. Postbuses in some areas have been used in this way, and hospital transport is also integrated into public transport in a few cases, (for example in the Borders Region of Scotland). Is it not possible that this principle could be extended to make better use of social work transport, either that which belongs to social work, or which is hired by it? My experience is that, informally, this may happen in some rural areas in respect of education transport. Day care transport could perhaps be combined with hired or public transport to shopping centres, and so on.

Inevitably, sheer physical distance and limited resources restrict the possibilities for providing special transport for all those who might otherwise make use of day care in rural areas. Some will be excluded for certain days of the week. For example, a study of three day centres for the elderly in Cambridgeshire[24] found that because one of the centres, Ely, served a more far-flung area than the other two, the department, with limited resources, could only provide transport to serve some areas on set days, thus limiting attendance. But this also had knock on effects:

> 'Support in the community relies on a combination of day care, domiciliary services and family or neighbour support (which itself may rely for its long-term continuance on the relief provided by day care attendance)'.

When attendance is restricted the restriction reduces relief afforded to helping neighbours and, in turn, places extra strain upon them. In time, this can strain the network to breaking point.

The Elderly in Rural Gloucestershire

A study of the use of services for the elderly in rural Gloucestershire[25] illustrates the interaction of various factors accounting for the population structure. There are too many elderly, including many who have settled there to retire from other areas, supported by too few younger people, partly because the younger people have left the region:

> 'The tourist's view of the Cotswolds ... is not a reality for many disadvantaged groups. Reality for them is an imbalance of population with the young leaving for employment ... cottages taken over for holiday weekends or commuter or retirement homes, inadequate public transport, shops, schools and post offices closed, and the increased cost of ... private transport. The elderly are particularly vulnerable.'

The study showed that the elderly living alone especially were tied to facilities in their own village - and that levels of provision inevitably showed great variation since social work day care provisions are seldom, if ever, conceived purely at a village level. Thus, out of 1,193 elderly or disabled people participating in the survey, only 12 attended lunch clubs, 39 attended day centres, 9 attended adult training centres and 3 attended sheltered workshops. These facilities were rarely available within the parish and often only open for a limited time each week.

The idea of mobile day services, analogous to mobile libraries, offers a way of tackling this problem to some extent, but it can be argued this is a second best to thinking of village-based services from a different starting point. Yet however radical the form of service delivery (for example working from a post office[24]) the necessity is to recognise the underlying question of what social services 'do' to a given specific locality, and what the features of that locality 'do' to the social services.

The Key Village Idea

A case study of a parish in North West Devon[27] describes the key village 'designed to consolidate village life and social welfare as a whole', but the evidence showed a lack of fit between this policy and other social policies affecting the area, based on other criteria. For most statutory services the key village was not a significant concept. The trend was for 'services to be provided from a town indiscriminately', and reflected planning opportunism as viewed from the towns. For example, a girls' hostel had been closed in the country town, Oakhampton so, for convenience, it became the distribution centre for meals on wheels. Subsequent reorganisation then made this centre serve not just the old borough but the whole surrounding countryside. In the process no particular notice was taken of the implications of the key village which was supposed to serve as the focal point for other relatively nearby villages, according to the philosophy of the key village. However the planning record was not altogether inimical to the development of the key village. The development of special housing for the elderly, for example, was sited specifically to take into account what the overall needs of the key village were.

During the course of the community studies forming part of my own research in the Highlands and Western Isles, I was impressed by a particular cooperative scheme in one remote area involving small scale industry. When I interviewed some of the members of the cooperative, however, it emerged that no particular thought had been given to the possibility of employing, for example, those in their own village who were mentally handicapped. Social workers should be aware of the need to link measures for community defence and development with their concerns as protectors of vulnerable groups. Yet the two interests can coalesce. A number of cooperative factories in Dunfermline were part of an initiative to develop training and employment opportunities partly for the mentally handicapped and partly for others in the locality without employment[16].

Social Network Patterns and Prevalence Rates for Children in Care

In discussing rural areas, special importance is always attached to the characteristic features of support from social networks. Grant, elsewhere in this issue, argues that 'the underlying pattern of differentiation in neighbourly care is similar within both urban and rural areas'. In other words the characteristic features of social networks depend on factors other than whether the client lives in an urban or rural setting. Irrespective of the setting, the Highlands and Western Isles study[16] postulated that there were two basic types of clients' social networks, the embracing type which seeks out and welcomes outside intervention and the self-contained type which resists it. These types can be found in all types of areas but the consequences and the implications are very different. In remote rural circumstances the embracing type is handicapped when physical factors such as transport and communication issues exacerbate other problems of rural living and come between expectations and their realisation. The self-contained type, on the other hand, may appear to function autonomously in such an area but if the quality of support is poor within that which is contained the consequences will be all the more detrimental. In its extreme form, to be socially imprisoned within an oppresive network is all the worse for being in a remote village. Such people may resemble the legendary 'skeletons in the village cupboard' as an SSRC research paper describes them[28].

If the notion of self-contained social networks is thought to be too nebulous as a general concept let us apply it to a specific issue e.g. children suffering or at risk from the alcohol problems of others. A local study in urban Lothian[29] found that out of a sample of 43 social work cases, 17 had alcohol related problems where, in aggregate, there were 43 children under sixteen living at home. What that experience meant to the children has unfortunately been traditionally regarded as part of alcohol studies more than as part of child care studies. But the alcohol problem, more privatised, but none the less severe, is known to be greater in some rural and remote areas than in the part of Lothian where the study took place. An alcohol related social network which included children at risk and was also more likely to be self-contained than embracing would be unlikely to come to the attention of the social worker in an area many miles from the nearest social work office. The hidden problem of the effects of alcohol on children at home is all the more hidden in some rural areas.

These sort of possibilities have to be taken into account in discussing the higher and lower rates of admissions of children into care, first brought out into the open many years ago by Packman and still a source of research and discussion[30][31].

Comparisons between prevalence rates for children in care must, of course, be treated with a good deal of circumspection. In the first place, the term 'in care' is not a valid indicator of the extent to which children are in residential care even if 'residential care' is extended to include fostering and adoption. Children technically 'in care' can reside with their parents; others who are not technically in care, in fact, reside away from home, especially if that takes, into consideration as it should, children in educational and health based establishments[13].

Nevertheless the authorities which chalked up the highest rates in Packman's study and which have continued to be high, as well as the low rates for most remote rural areas, are still a source of interest and sometimes embarrassment[30]. The rate varies from over 28 per 1000 of the general population aged 0-17 to under 2 per 1000. The reasons are still not fully understood although they must include differences in policies, expectations and levels of provision. They may also reflect differences in kinds of networks.

To take an example: the Lothian study suggested links between child care problems and alcoholism. We know that alcoholism is a problem in remote areas as well as in some urban areas and we can expect child care problems related to alcoholism in rural as well as in urban areas. If the alcohol-related social network is self-contained the risk to children may be less evident to the 'authorities' which in turn could affect demand for admission to care.

If Grant is right in arguing that informal caring networks are to be found in both urban and rural areas, we still need a more refined analysis of different kinds of networks affecting people in different specific localities, not necessarily based on an urban/ rural distinction. Such an analysis could contribute some insight into the relationship of types of social networks and rates of admission to care.

The difference in levels of provision in urban and rural areas is complicated by the fact that, until recently at least the urban areas with the high rates traditionally shipped many of their children out into the rural areas or into other towns with lower rates[33]. Some still do[8], yet because of an absence of local facilities in some remote areas, the few children that had to be sent away - often through educational rather than social work channels - were themselves displaced to places far removed from their homes[13]. The implication of this for children coming from homes with different cultural features, as well as being in varying degrees embracing or self-contained in type, may be imagined. From the point of view of sustaining and enhancing concern and social care for children through informal supporting networks in their local communities, it now seems little short of scandalous that only a few years ago, for example, handicapped children from the remote Highlands could be ensconced in the centre of Glasgow, because of the absence of placements considered suitable nearer at hand, while children from central Glasgow were removed to the nethermost northern regions in the interests of the alleged benefits that would accrue.

Children are less often today placed in a rural residential setting through choice. In practice it is suspected that many existing children's homes and other children's establishments, as well as hospitals, are still out of town because the barnacle effect unforgettably described by Carlbach[34] still counts in this respect. In the case of large conurbations like London involving different local authorities, such arrangements inhibit the fulfilment of child care policies based on greater localisation of provisions and less fragmentation of kinds of residential care.

One aspect of localisation is the placement of children within the locality in order that they can more easily return to their home surroundings or at least to a familiar environment for fostering (where going home is impractical). The current evaluation of a children's home I have been engaged in, based on such policies, illustrates the need for back-up community services if it is to succeed in the rural community in which it is placed[35].

It is doubtful whether there will ever be a single policy for residential care. For example, as far as children are concerned long-term milieu approaches to education and care are likely to be juxtaposed with the possibilities for short-term intervention with the intention of returning children to their home environments as soon as possible. It is necessary to sustain and maximise the advantages of different policies as offering practical choices rather than seeing them in competition. One choice may suit one type of network, bearing in mind different implications in different kinds of areas.

Research into these questions should help policy makers and practitioners to understand more fully the basis of the choices they can make with their clients. More research is needed to do this.

The relationship between social networks and the elderly in care also involves new kinds of considerations from a few years ago. Privatisation, for example, appears as a new development. This may favour certain kinds of communities which include suburbanised rural areas or coastal locations[12]. In the long run such developments could affect the pattern of residential services but it is too early to say. For example, is it clear whether the clientele of such establishments are new to the private sector? Some of them might otherwise have been in the long-standing hidden group of elderly making use of guest houses or hotels rather than having to undergo a formal admission to Part III accommodation. Private provision for disturbed children also appears to be on the increase taking advantage of the shift to more purposeful aims in the use of residential provision. Advocates of private provision claim it offers greater flexibility - an argument traditionally associated with voluntary initiatives[12].

SUMMARY

We have looked briefly at the sorts of issues that are thrown up by relating residential and day care policies and practice to the urban and rural dimension of current societal changes. These issues have been discussed around three themes: localisation, integrating the planning and responsive components to social service provision and the relationship between social work policies and community development in the broadest sense of taking into account global social and economic forces as they apply to specific locations. Largely local or regional research findings have been used to illustrate how these themes interrelate and justify a broad perspective in considering residential and day care policy and practice. Such a perspective must take into account, for example the use of different kinds of informal networks which may be characterised as 'embracing' or as 'self-contained' each of which will have different implications for intervention in different environments.

The conclusion to be drawn from what little research is available is that it is worthwhile examining issues surrounding residential and day care in rural terms because this will highlight the need for more integrated, more localised and more responsive approaches. Positive solutions that are found in rural areas may then be of interest to some urban areas.

References

1. Finberg, J. Exploring Villages. Routledge, 1958, p. 236.
2. S.C.S.S. Residential Facilities in Scotland, Annual Directories 1978-1983.
3. Hunt, L. The Changing Role of Social Work - An Organisational Study. (Unpublished thesis) Aberdeen University, Social Work Department, 1984.
4. Lishman, J. (Ed.) Developing Services for the Elderly. Research Highlights No. 3, University of Aberdeen Social Work Department, 1982.
5. Reinach, E. (Ed.) Decision Making in Child Care. Research Highlights No. 1, University of Aberdeen Social Work Department, 1981.
6. Reinach, E. (Ed.) Normalisation. Research Highlights No. 2, University of Aberdeen Social Work Department, 1981
7. Lishman, J. (Ed.) Social Work with Adult Offenders. Research Highlights No. 5, University of Aberdeen Social Work Department, 1983.
8. Strathclyde Regional Council Director of Social Work. Home or Away? Residential Child Care Strategy for the Eighties. Strathclyde Regional Council Social Work Department, (undated).

9. Carter, J. Day Services for Adults: Somewhere to Go. Allen & Unwin, 1981.
10. King, M. 'Research into Residential Care' Decision Making in Child Care. Research Highlights No. 1, University of Aberdeen Social Work Department, 1981.
11. Fiddes, B. Review of the Future of List D Schools - Summary of Findings and Conclusions. Chadwick Healey, 1983. For a critical review see also Forrest, A.R. 'Dispute over values cannot be settled by recourse to arithmetic' The Scottish Child. January, 1984.
12. Murray, N. 'Privates on Parade' Community Care. March 8, 1984, 18-21.
13. Seed, P. & Thomson, M. All Kinds of Care. Scottish Academic Press, 1978.
14. Glastonbury, B. et al. Social Work in Conflict. BASW, 1983. (Croom Helm, 1981).
15. Shaw, M. & Stockford, D. 'The Role of Statutory Agencies in Rural Areas: Planning and Social Services' in Shaw, M. (Ed.) Rural Deprivation and Planning. University of East Anglia, 1979.
16. Seed, P. et al. Mental Handicap in the Highlands and Western Isles. Detailed Report to Sponsors. University of Aberdeen Department of Social Work, 1980.
17. Seed, P. Mental Handicap: Who Helps in Rural and Remote Communities? Costello, 1980.
18. Raddery School, Fortrose, Ross-shire. Principal: David Dean.
19. Walton, R. G. Social Work 2000 - The Future of Social Work in a Changing Society. Longman, 1982.
20. Jones, H. 'Some Factors in Third World Social Policy' Social Policy and Administration. Vol 17, No. 2, Summer, 1983.
21. Rosie, G. 'The Cromarty Firth' in Maxwell, S. (Ed.) Scotland, Multi-Nationals and the Third World. Mainstream Publishing, Edinburgh, 1982.
22. Moore, R. The Social Impact of Oil: The Case of Peterhead. Routledge, 1982.
23. Suffolk County Council. 'Stowmarket Social Education Centre - The First Year of Operation - Detailed Report' Clearing House for Social Services Research. University of Birmingham, Department of Social Administration, No. 1, 1983.
24. Cambridgeshire Social Services Department. 'Elderly Users of Day Care' Clearing House for Social Services Research.

University of Birmingham, Department of Social Administration, No. 6, 1981.

25. Westley, P. & Ewans, S. 'England's Green and Not so Pleasant Land' Community Care. October 20, 1983.
26. White, J. 'Everywhere in Chains?' Social Work Today. Vol. 12, No. 48, August 12, 1981.
27. Glyn-Jones, A. Rural Recovery: Has it Begun? Devon County Council and University of Exeter, 1979.
28. Social Science Research Council. Way of Life: Negative Aspects of Community. North Sea Panel, Occasional Paper No. 8 (undated).
29. Lothian Regional Council. 'Alcohol-Related Problems in Current Social Work Cases (Summary)' Clearing House for Social Services Research. University of Birmingham, Department of Social Administration, No. 6, 1981.
30. Packman, J. Child Care Needs and Numbers. Allen & Unwin, 1968.
31. Social Work Services Group. Statistical Bulletin - Children in Care or Under Supervision as at 31.3.83. Government Statistical Service.
32. London Borough of Tower Hamlets. 'Why Does Tower Hamlets Have as Many Children in Care?' Clearing House for Local Authority Social Services Research. Birmingham University, Department of Social Administration, No. 3, 1982.
33. Ferguson, T. Children in Care - and After. OUP, 1966.
34. Carlbach, J. Caring for Children in Trouble. Routledge, 1970.
35. University of Aberdeen, Social Work Department. The Evaluation of a Children's Home with New Child Care Policies. SSRC Collaborative Project with Grampian Regional Council Social Work Department.

RURAL/URBAN DIFFERENCES IN HEALTH CARE: SOME RESEARCH EVIDENCE

Gillian Dalley

INTRODUCTION

This paper looks at the extent of research evidence for the existence of rural/urban differences in health care from a number of perspectives. It also attempts to assess what implications the existence of any differences may have for practitioners involved in the delivery of health care and personal social services.

While there is a growing body of work relating to the geographical distribution of health care, much of it tends to look only at regional differences and does not break them down into rural/urban categories. Thus there may be marked differences between one region and another but it is often impossible to deduce from the available data how far these may be characterised as urban/rural differences or not since all regions are composed of rural and urban populations in varying proportions. However, there are a number of studies which do contain data on the urban/rural dimension and these tend to fall broadly into two categories - studies of the distribution of health care provision on the one hand, and studies of the utilisation of services on the other.

The work comes from a variety of sources, and the conceptual frameworks, methodology and aims of these various works tend to vary considerably. Four broad approaches seem to emerge. First, there is the approach which locates discussion of health care differences within the overall poverty debate, suggesting that lack of access to and under-utilisation of health services in rural areas form part of a generalised rural deprivation[1], which extends from transport, education, personal social services and health care, through to the overall cost of living and widespread lack of knowledge about rights and services[2]. Second, there is the service providers' approach which is concerned with assessing how far a service is being utilised and, to a lesser extent, the degree of consumer satisfaction [3][4]. A survey methodology is generally employed. Rural/urban differences may emerge from the results almost incidentally as one of many findings, or occasionally (as in the case of the Consumer Council - commissioned surveys[4][5][6]) be the basis for the commissioning of the survey. Third, there are the attempts by geographers to construct rational spatial planning models which aim at maximising accessibility[7][8] and efficiency in resource allocation. Their techniques are applicable both in rural and urban contexts and differences between them are those of degree rather than quality. Fourth is an approach which tends to be concerned with qualitative differences between town and country for both patients and practitioners alike; such studies are usually small-scale investigations of attitudes to and subjective experiences of localised forms of health care[9][10]. Of course, some studies may combine elements of several of these different approaches, and it cannot be assumed that they are mutually exclusive. Two major themes underlie most studies: the problems of accessibility and utilisation. Clearly, there is a third major problem, that of need, which should inform any study of the other problems but the issue of how to define need is problematic. Planners involved in resource allocation, for example, RAWP and SHARE[11][12] have attempted to deal with the problem of need by regarding morbidity and mortality figures as proxy indicators of need (notably the SMR, Standard Mortality Ratio) but it is generally recognised that there is no absolute indicator for 'need for health care'[13]. In any case morbidity and mortality figures are rarely broken down beyond regional level into rural/urban categories and so are not available anyway for the purpose of this review. And it can be argued that 'need' is a concept far too complex to be measured in the way that planners have adopted in the past. In the rural/urban context, critics would suggest that subjective perceptions of need will influence the degree of felt need and expressed need found in a population and that because rural populations tend to have self-reliant, stoical views of their life circumstances this leads to an under-estimation of their need. The subject is too complex to be addressed satisfactorily in this paper but the issue should always be borne in mind when any consideration of service provision and utilisation is undertaken.

There is one further issue to be addressed in this Introduction and that is in relation to how the terms rural and urban are defined and used. There is no single usage and it is necessary to remember this if any comparison is attempted. Some studies[1] base their terminology on local government definitions used before the 1974 reorganisation - that is, the rural district and the urban district[14]. However, urban districts as then defined could also include remote and isolated areas, such as the highest fells in the Lake District (part of the Lakes Urban District)[1]. Conversely, rural districts could be categorised into various different types: truly rural (both sparsely populated remote upland areas and intensively-farmed lowland areas), predominantly rural (commuter areas surrounding large cities and industrial areas) and predominantly non-rural (continuously built-up areas around large towns and cities). Walker complains that there are too few data available on these forms of settlement patterns on which cost-effective planning can be based.

Some studies base their terminology on a modification of the rural district/urban district distincton. The OPCS survey[3] uses this distinction but adds 'interviewer's assessment' and ward density as other factors to take into account. Other studies regard 'remoteness' as a more important measure than the straightforward rural/urban dichotomy. But an area can be remote in an absolute sense[4] - like the Scottish Highlands or the Cumbrian fells - or it can be remote in a relative sense - like the villages in East Anglia studied by Haynes and Bentham[15] which are regarded as remote in relation to other villages which are closer to Norwich and better served. There is then an additional fact to consider - small country towns in 'absolutely' remote areas which are the local service centres of their rural hinterland may also be designated rural in comparison with large cities which may dominate a whole region (for example, Elgin, as opposed to Aberdeen, in Grampian Region, or Oban, as opposed to Glasgow, in Strathclyde Region). In this sense, 'rural' is being defined in relation to degrees of service centralisation.

The paper is divided into three sections: the first looks at a group of studies which is concerned with the general problem of accessibility and utilisation employing a variety of methodologies;

the second is concerned with similar problems but uses a specific methodology - spatial planning models; the third section looks at the approach employed in small-scale, qualitative studies.

ACCESSIBILITY AND UTILISATION

Although it was noted earlier that the problem of estimating levels of need for health care in a given population was extremely difficult, a paper by Tudor Hart[16] in 1971, attempting to deal with that problem, has proved influential in the related area of accessibility and utilisation studies. Tudor Hart proposed, on the basis of large and continuing social and geographical inequalities in morbidity and mortality rates, that the availability of good medical care varies inversely with the need for care in the population being served. 'The force that creates and maintains the inverse care law', he argues ' is the operation of the market, and its cultural and ideological superstructure which has permeated the thought and directed the ambitions of our profession'. Although the problem of defining need beyond the use of morbidity and mortality rates is not tackled, Tudor Hart's proposition has been used as the starting point for many later studies concerned with assessing accessibility to and utilisation of health care. Accessibility and utilisation have to be seen as key components of the unequal distribution of health care resources leading to inequalities in the health standards of different groups in the population[17]. Most studies of lack of access and under-utilisation are concerned with the problem faced by inner-city, working class populations[18], and tend not to deal with conditions in the rural areas.

The conference convened by CPAG on rural poverty in 1978 can be seen as an attempt to draw the rural context into studies of poverty and deprivation. Walker's introduction to the collection of papers presented at the conference[19] provides a good overview of the nature of rural deprivation and Heller's paper on health care in rural areas[20] takes the view that deprivation in health terms can be seen as lack of access to health care due to a number of factors: transport difficulties (high cost and inadequacy), shortages of medical facilities and the centralisation of services away from rural areas. He cites a National Federation of Women's Institutes

Survey[21] which found that of 226 settlements with populations of less than 500, 87% had no doctor's surgery, 99% had no chemist and 100% had no dentist or optician. In addition, where there were surgeries, the quality was poor (surgeries only open for short periods, no toilet facilities, restricted types of service - for minor ailments or children only and so forth). The groups most likely to suffer in terms of access, and therefore most likely to exhibit an inabilitiy to utilise the resources were women with young children, working class people and the elderly, precisely those categories with the bulk of mortality and excess morbidity. Such groups in rural areas were also likely to be multiply deprived in terms of lacking a telephone, non-ownership of a car, no local bus service, low income, and so on.

He also makes the point that while the DHSS has made an attempt at a more equitable distribution through the RAWP (and SHARE, in Scotland) formula, it has neglected to take account of the extra costs involved in providing services in rural areas, and has tended to concentrate on inner-city problems. Most attempts at geographical redistribution stop at the regional level, and fail to look at the more specific contexts of rural/urban differences[22].

Surveys relating to accessibility and utilisation generally deal with the provision of primary care, mostly GP services. Haynes and Bentham's study of health care in East Anglia[15] is more unusual in that it looks at GP consultations, out-patient referrals <u>and</u> hospital admissions contrasting five geographical categories - ranging from areas within the city, villages close to the city with and without a GP surgery, and villages far from the city with and without a GP surgery. They are concerned to see how far these factors of remoteness and availability of facilities affect consultation and referral rates, and how far the variables of age and social class intervene.

They found that there were marked differences between respondents with a longstanding illness and those without. In those with long-standing illness there were marked differences between urban and rural (all categories) respondents, with urban dwellers making use of the GP and out-patient services to a greater extent than rural folk. There was a tendency for the balance to be redressed at the hospital admissions stage and it may be that hospital doctors are aware of the inhibiting effect of rural dwelling at earlier stages in the consultation procedure. Manual workers and the elderly were less likely to make use of the services than other categories with longstanding illness.

Of those without any longstanding illness, young, mobile (car-owning) and relatively well-off people living in relatively accessible villages tended to make greater use of the services than those from other locations. This indicated perhaps that they have higher expectations of the health service than other groups, and this is confirmed by examining responses to two questions designed to test attitudes of self-reliance and expectations. In contrast, the findings for people with a longstanding illness suggest that there are no differences between urban and rural populations in expectations or degrees of self-reliance - which runs counter to views expressed many times elsewhere that rural people have lower expectations of the services and make fewer demands on the services because of greater stoicism[9].

Haynes and Bentham compare their findings with other studies notably of Cumbria[5], South Wales[6] and Scotland[4] as well as with a national UK survey[3]. The Scottish study, commissioned by the Scottish Consumer Council, found a similar tendency for the remoteness of a location to affect attendance at out-patient clinics and to create problems of access to GPs. These latter problems were moderated, however, partly because of the higher ratio of GPs to patients exhibited in the Western Isles (where the study took place) in comparison with rural areas elsewhere in the UK and partly, the study suggests, because district nurses took on some functions of the GP in the more distant areas. Chiropody and dental services were, however, much more difficult to obtain in the remoter locations. Interestingly, while the authors suggest that there may be some limited confirmation of the inverse care law (especially in relation to the care of the elderly), they feel that the services in general make compensatory efforts to prevent the exacerbation of its working, which would otherwise have been expected given the remoteness of the area.

The Cumbria and South Wales studies failed to find evidence of any marked problems of access in either area, except for a minority of elderly people in Cumbria, but Haynes and Bentham question whether the sampling design of either survey was adequate for such problems to be shown up.

Wenger[9], though, in a study conducted in North Wales did not find any greater problems of access either, since a majority were car-users and did not have to rely on public transport (which was poor and costly). But she recognised the phenomenon of 'forced car-ownership'[23] and saw that in terms of comparative disadvantage this was a factor to take into account. Both Wenger and the Western Isles study regarded local attitudes as important factors in any discussion of access and utilisation and this will be considered later in this paper.

The most comprehensive survey of accessibility is the OPCS survey conducted by Ritchie, Jacoby and Bone[3], which looks at access to primary care throughout the UK. This includes all primary care services - GP consultations, location of surgeries, administration of practices, district nursing services, health visiting, pharmacies and dispensing services, chiropody, dental and opthalmic services. The survey was commissioned by the UK health departments because of the renewed emphasis on the importance of community health care and the provision of care by integrated health care teams as outlined in various discussion documents in the 1970's[24][25], along with trends to organise teams within single locations, in group practices and in health centres. The researchers were interested in the age, sex and social class of the sample, together with measures of 'aids to access' (such things as possession of cars and telephones, contacts with neighbours and so on). Many of the data were broken down into rural and non-rural categories, so it is possible to determine how far any differences between the two categories were exhibited. There was a greater personal use of cars in rural areas than non-rural areas (53%:37%) but no difference in telephone ownership (62% and 64% having telephones). These geographical differences were cross cut by social class and compounded by age - 72% of social class V as compared to 10% of social class I having no car, and 70%:9% having no telephone. In terms of GP services, people in rural areas were less likely to be on single handed practice lists (except in rural areas in Scotland and Wales, where they were more likely), or on lists of more than 2500 patients. In general the rural population had to travel further to the surgery than non-rural patients (e.g. less than 1 mile : 33% rural; 54% non-rural; between 2-5 miles: 36% rural; 15% non-rural). Ninety per cent of respondents felt it was easy to get to see their GP, but the findings show that being on a large list and living some distance from the surgery seemed to have a 'slight deterrent effect' on consultation rates. Older people, although they found it more difficult to get to the surgery expressed a high level of satisfaction, especially on the availability of home visits, while there was a tendency for mothers with young children to have found difficulty in obtaining a home visit, but there was no difference between rural and non/rural areas in these responses.

While Ritchie et al[3] seem to suggest that the general level of satisfaction with GP services was high, they point out in their summary that a rate of 10-15% of dissatisfaction represents 2,000,000 people on a country-wide basis, which is not a small number. They also conclude that age, sex and social class together with levels of personal mobility and access were more important variables than a straightforward rural/ non-rural dichotomy.

Turning to some of the other primary care services, any difficulties in access to pharmacies were lessened for rural patients by the fact that many more rural doctors dispensed drugs themselves than did their non-rural counterparts. Fifteen per cent of rural respondents found pharmacists difficult to get to, as compared with 4% of non-rural respondents, but 20% of the rural sample had dispensing GPs.

Unfortunately, the data on health visiting and district nursing services are not broken down into rural and non-rural categories so it is difficult to form any picture of the provision of these services according to area. Indeed, there seems to be very little research available at all that looks at rural/urban differences for health visiting and community nursing. The Western Isles study[4] comments on the intermediate role of the district nurse in some of the remoter islands and Haynes and Bentham raise the matter in their East Anglia study[15]. They raise a rather different point, however; they suggest that the reason why urban patients with a long-standing illness tend to consult the GP more often than non-urban patients might be because the ancillary primary care services are more developed within the city and therefore facilitate contact with the GP. However, Wenger[9] and the Western Isles study suggest that contacts with the ancillary services are as well developed in rural areas as in urban areas, so the Haynes and Bentham hypothesis is not confirmed. Indeed, it is possible that both tendencies exist - in urban areas the ancillary services acting as facilitators of GP contacts and in rural areas as substitutes.

There is a small reference to the role of health visiting in rural areas in a report by Robinson[26] examining the feasibility of conducting an evaluative study of health visiting. In a preliminary study, intended as a pilot for a larger study, she found that attendance at the Paediatric Development Clinic (when a baby was 6 weeks old) was poorer for infants resident in urban parishes than for those in rural parishes. This she found surprising in the light of two earlier reports[27],[28], which described difficulties which rural mothers experienced in attending child health clinics. These two reports (the first in 1946 and the second in 1978) were separated by thirty years, but both identified similar problems, so Robinson concluded that her own finding should not be regarded as necessarily valid; she recommended replication of her study on a much larger scale in order for her findings to be validated.

Two further points should be considered before concluding this section on accessibility and utilisation. First, it should be noted that accessibility is a factor to be taken into account in both rural and urban contexts. The last two decades have seen a substantial trend for doctors to cluster together in group practices and in health centres. Ritchie et al found that there had been a tendency for distance to GP surgery to increase for urban patients due to the growth of group practices (though not due to the development of health centres). In addition, several sources[8][29] mention the difficulty of access which some working class populations have in terms of poor public transport facilities; others[18] discuss the failure of the 'designated area' policy to redress the balance in GP under-provision in innner-city areas (characterised by a greater concentration of elderly single-handed GPs).

Second, it should be noted that while there may be distinctive rural/urban differences in some aspects of health care there are also distinctive differences <u>between</u> different rural areas. The obvious difference is the distribution and type of general practices in rural areas in Scotland and Wales as compared to rural areas elsewhere. Practice lists tend to be smaller and there are a larger number of rural single handed practices in these two areas. Qualitative studies such as the study by Horobin and McIntosh[10][30] show how very different a rural single-handed practice in parts of Scotland is from single-handed practices elsewhere. There is some evidence to suggest that levels of expectation and degrees of satisfaction may also vary between rural areas. Intra-rural differences may be attributable to a variety of reasons - national reasons, differences in 'rural-ness' (remote, sparsely populated/ lowland intensively farmed), regional resource allocation inequalities and so on. There is little evidence to show which may be the most likely. But the differences exist.

SPATIAL PLANNING MODELS

There is a body of work, mostly produced by medical geographers, which is concerned with constructing spatial planning models on which an equitable and rational allocation of health service resources can be based. They are particularly concerned with the location of particular resources such as health centres, hospitals, GP surgeries and so on in optimum positions in terms of patient accessibility and service efficiency. The aims and methodology of their technique is applicable to both urban and rural contexts. Knox[8], for example, applied the techniques to the distribution of GP surgeries in Aberdeen, examining changes in their location area over time. He suggests that between 1950 and 1970, in spite of NHS attempts at a more equitable and accessible distribution of GP services, the location of surgeries still persists in favouring middle class districts of the city. He is able to compute accessibility using mathematical formulae and demonstrates how steeply levels of accessibility fall off with distance from a small highly favoured core area (the 'distance-decay parameter'). He cites this in support of the Tudor Hart inverse care law, commenting that the 'inaccessibility of primary care facilities may be seen as yet another layer of relative deprivation, reinforcing the geography of urban socio-economic malaise as well as further intensifying the cycle of poverty'.

Joseph and Bantock[7] use the same techniques for measuring accessibilty to GPs in rural areas in Canada. They see this as crucial for the delivery of health care, since, they argue, the GP is the key referral agent to other levels of the health care system given the increasing development of 'facility based' treatment as compared to 'home based' treatment. They see the urban orientation of medicine as one of the reasons for the relative scarcity of rural GPs in Canada, and use their techniques to demonstrate the disparities between urban and rural services.

The spatial analysis of surgery locations is also examined by Curtis[31]; she suggests alternative procedures in measuring the availability of GP services, by an analysis of travel distance for the service population, rather than by simple distance. She says that the 'friction of distance' can be significant in the selection of GPs by patients. She applies the procedure by applying different weights to various groups in the service population, taking into account needs and levels of morbidity.

The work of Smith[32], and Eyles, Smith and Woods[33] represents a more critical approach in this field; Smith suggests that geographers have a tendency to search for hierarchical structures in the spatial organisation of health services ('central place theory') and says that it is important to recognise two conflicting forces which are operating against each other at the same time: centripetal forces for centralisation and concentration of resources in the interests of efficiency and centrifugal forces in the interests of equity. While there is some evidence to show that those living closest to facilities make the greater use of them, and that it is tempting to see this as an outcome of spatial process (distance decay) within a system of hierarchically structured spatial organisation, it is also important to remember that this is not an outcome merely of generalised spatial inequality but of a particular conception of health care (i.e. hospital-and medically-dominated facilities, high-technology, and so on). He suggests that it is necessary to look at the spatial distribution of illness and the spatial arrangement of the health services as part of the interrelationship between particular forms of economic, political and social structures in society.

Eyles et al[33] take this view as a starting point, and show how the techniques of spatial resource allocation planning are based on certain narrow assumptions - specifically, that resource allocation is a technical problem 'capable of resolution by the application of rational criteria to decide the relative need of people in different territories, leading to judgements on which territories should receive more or less resources'. It goes on to examine RAWP's and the London Hospital Planning Consortium's plans for health care in London, and criticises them on the basis that class inequalities and the nature of the capitalist state all impose limitations on and problems in this approach to planning.

Coupland[29] in a paper on class and gender pursues some of these points, suggesting that geographical access to resources depends on two inter-related factors, namely the location of the individual relative to the facility in question and the individual's personal mobility. She looks in particular at the failure of some working class women with young children to take up community health facilities in inner-city areas. She sees the encumbrance of young children as a limiting factor on women's mobility. While she is referring to inner-city areas, the point is applicable to both urban and rural contexts.

Whether or not there can be such a thing as objective rational planning, given the criticisms which Smith and colleagues make, Mohan[34] suggests that the authorities who are in a position to implement such plans often fail to make use of them anyway. He describes how a Regional Health Authority and an Area Health Authority in north-east England were at loggerheads over the implementation of location-allocation plans which the AHA had drawn-up. In the end, the RHA won the argument, and Mohan suggests that local interests (especially those which take rural needs into account) will always get overlooked. He goes on to question how far technical planning can be valid without an adequate theory of the state. Grime and Whitelegg[22] take up the theme of how difficult it is to reconcile local planning needs with national planning models.

To conclude this section, it is clear that the approach which geographers have developed (and criticised) has some relevance to the consideration of rural and urban differences especially in terms of attempts to redistribute resources more equitably on a spatial basis. The move to incorporate less narrowly technical-rational considerations into location-allocation models - taking into account age, gender, social class and mobility/accessibility factors - is especially relevant.

INTENSIVE SMALL-SCALE STUDIES

Wenger's study on the elderly in the community in N. Wales[9], although primarily a social services research project, contains interesting and useful data on the provision of health care for the elderly in several rural communities. In general, her conclusions about levels of provision are positive and do not confirm the rural deprivation thesis. Part of her research was conducted in interviews with a sample of 688 elderly people living in 8 rural communities; during the course of interview, they were asked about home visits received from health and social service professionals. In comparison with a UK survey conducted by Hunt[35] of the elderly at home, they scored substantially higher for visits from district nurses (18:8) and ministers (50:16) with very similar scores for visits from health visitors (5:4), home helps (8:9), social workers (6:5), meals on wheels (7:3) and voluntary organisations (3:3). They scored less for home visits from doctors (28:33) but the proportion for those living alone was the same in rural Wales as it was for the UK (28:28) [% home visits received from professionals in preceding 6 months].

She suggests that while the literature on rural deprivation (which she cites extensively) is persuasive, the argument is not proven in the case of the communities she studied in N. Wales. She found that public transport was generally poor, but that the level of car ownership was compensatorily high; she found that domiciliary support services were well established and equal to or higher than elsewhere; she found that there was general satisfaction with accessibility to post offices, doctors' surgeries and food shops (although she does not give any figures for the cost of food and other goods in local shops as compared with costs of goods in urban shops. In terms of self-assessment, the health of the rural elderly seemed no worse than of those living in towns and in terms of self-reliance and insistence on doing things for themselves, the rural elderly scored much more highly. There was a general satisfaction with the 'rural way of life' which compensated for any lack of amenities which might be associated with rural living (for example, lack of plumbing, distance between houses or settlements). Wenger emphasises the importance of cultural attitudes in assessing the situation of rural populations and stresses that the spirit of co-operation which seemed to exist in these communities was a very important factor to take into account (good neighbours, farmers using tractors to get doctors through to snow-bound houses, helpful shopkeepers, postmen, milkmen and so on). She does, however, suggest that the cost of living is high (especially given the fact of lower rural incomes) and that the nutritional values of the diets of the rural elderly may be poor through lack of fresh foods. Unfortunately, there are no data given on access to hospital services (both out-patient and in-patient services), although Wenger mentions there is no district general hospital, and that the only psychiatric hospital is in Denbigh, serving the whole of North Wales. So it is difficult to assess how far the rural communities which she studied can be said to be deprived in terms of access to centralised facilities.

The study by Bloor, Horobin, Taylor and Williams[4] on the Western Isles consisted of interviews with 319 people living in 6 different locations in the Western Isles, varying in degrees of distance from Stornoway, the main town (where 60 were interviewed).

In terms of per capita spending, the population of the Western Isles is not under-provided for (Western Isles Health Board spending is in the mid-range for Scottish Health Boards); the GP ratio is highly favourable (list size: 1,435 as compared to Scotland: 1,928 and England: 2,365); they have the tenth highest number of medical and ancillary staff per 1000 population and one community nurse to 492 persons as compared to the overall Scottish ratio of 1:1259. In terms of hospital admissions for the elderly, they are well below average though, and similarly for out-patient referrals for children.

In their discussion of their findings, Bloor er al suggest that a distinction between distance and remoteness can be made. Remoteness can have two attributes in this context - geographical remoteness (in part defined by distance) and also in relation to the manner in which health service resources are distributed. In terms of remoteness to the distribution of resources (i.e. acccessibility), barriers to equal access can be determined by a number of factors as well as geography - social class inequalities, hazardous home environments, dangerous occupations and so on. In addition, they note, similar barriers to equal access to the distribution of other, non-health services may exist, which may lead to extra demands and burdens being placed upon the health service (they include such things as poor housing, controls over air pollution and insufficient safeguards against industrial diseases).

This argument is one which is rehearsed in sources discussed earlier in the paper, and points to the fact that a straightforward rural/urban dichotomy is not necessarily the appropriate conceptual categorisation to make, and that it may be cross cut by many other factors.

Both Wenger's[9] and Bloor et al's[4] studies emphasis the particular importance of a population's attitudes to the provision of health care. Bloor et al suggest that there is a widespread Hebridean scepticism about mainland values and that it is important to investigate local definitions of need. For example, while in the most remote area (South Uist) it took longer and cost more to travel to the surgery, it was only the cost that was seen to be a problem. The time factor was disregarded. Another example was cited in the case of the wearing of false teeth. Fewer people in the more distant areas were troubled about failure to obtain well-fitting false teeth or repairs to them when broken. This was because while teeth may be seen as an aid to appearance, 'aids to appearance were not highly valued in a society where there are few strangers on whom a good impression is required'. In addition, it appeared that greater value was given to dying and being born within the community rather than being taken to hospital. Thus, in the case of the elderly, more illnesses were coped with at home than elsewhere because this was valued, regardless of the fact that access to a hospital was, in any case, difficult. Thus remoteness, in some instances, may not be the causal factor.

Seed's work on mental handicap[36] touches on the differences in cultural values and attitudes which may be exhibited in rural areas. He found that in many instances families with mentally handicapped members could be seen as deprived in terms of service provision - he cites poor public transport, together with a lower incidence of car ownership, leading to restricted social networks, poor educational facilities and restricted access to employment. He suggests that it is possible that in areas where the prevalence of mental handicap is highest there are the fewest services available and he points out the key part which families and relatives play in caring for the mentally handicapped in rural areas.

He goes on to discuss how there is no uniform perception of mental handicap in rural communities, but that in some parts of the Highlands and Islands, community attitudes of tolerance and acceptance seemed to exist which recognised the rights of mentally handicapped people to be respected and which saw that they had a role to play in the life of the local community. In fact, the conditions of rural life seemed to foster this in the sense it was often easier for mentally handicapped people to find 'employment' working in crofting and other informally organised jobs than for their urban counterparts.

Professional attitudes to the rural dimension of work are discussed in two papers by Horobin and McIntosh[10][30]; they contrast the conceptual views of time which rural and urban GPs have. For the rural practitioner, they suggest that time is not viewed as a scarce resource (reminiscent of the attitudes of Western Isles patients) and that they gained a great deal of satisfaction from being able to work steadily, in an unpressurised fashion, in conditions and surroundings which they enjoyed. In addition, rural GPs felt able to spend time dealing with patients' social problems, and did not view them as time wasters. They exhibited respect for their rural patients, praising their stoical and sturdy self-reliance. Urban GPs, however, felt they worked under pressure and that consequently there was always the risk of cutting corners leading to faulty diagnosis. Risks for rural GPs were perceived as the absence of a safety-net of specialist advice and facilities as back-up.

Evidence from the qualitative studies described above, then, seems to substantiate the view that there is a difference in cultural attitudes between town and country and that this does affect perceptions of need and willingness to adapt to absence of facilities. The existence of objectively defined deprivation in rural areas is, however, problematic. In certain respects it may be said to exist (cost of living; Western Isles and, perhaps, Welsh in-patient and out-patient rates; distances to be travelled), but in other respects it is not proven (domiciliary support in Wales; district nursing and GP services in the Western Isles).

IMPLICATIONS FOR PRACTITIONERS

From the evidence reviewed in this paper, it is difficult to point to any clear implications for practitioners either in health or social work. Horobin and McIntosh[30] make reference to the fact that a number of rural GPs expressed resentment of newly attached social workers who, they felt, were taking over some of their role as 'family doctors', i.e. their role as counsellors as well as clinicians. Dingwall[37], in a paper on health visiting, describes how the district nursing officer insisted on restricting her health visitors to medically-defined problems while the health visitors themselves tended to blame restrictions on intrusions from social workers. Seed[36], in his work on mental handicap, discusses the possibility of creating a unified service (including health, education and social work) but feels more research into the feasibility of such a scheme should be undertaken before implementation; in any case, equally important would be the need to integrate professional and community effort. In current research which Hunter[38] is undertaking, there is evidence in some areas of health visitors and district nurses sharing responsibilities, although this is not repeated in neighbouring areas within the same Health Board district. Evidence from the Western Isles shows that there is a successful sharing of responsibilities between GPs and district nurses. In my own current research[39], I have found the divisions and antipathy which Horobin et al and Dingwall mention between health workers and social workers are exhibited in rural areas as well as in urban contexts. Given the increasing emphasis on community care and on the development of multi-disciplinary primary care teams, it is an unfortunate finding. It is essential that collaboration and co-operation be developed for these policies to be implemented successfully. It seems that such co-operation may well be possible within each service (health/social work) but more difficult to achieve between services.

CONCLUSION

This paper has considered how far the application of a rural/urban categorisation is valid in the field of health care provision. In some senses, notably the area of cultural attitudes, levels of satisfaction and perceptions of need, the evidence seems to suggest that there is a difference between 'town' and 'country'. But the evidence also shows how difficult it is to construct separate conceptual categories to be labelled rural and urban.

In terms of service provision and accessibility to services, much of the location-allocation data and the data gained from large scale surveys seem to confirm that rural populations (however defined) are at a disadvantage in comparison with urban populations. However, much of the qualitative data, based on small-scale intensive studies, suggest that this disadvantage is not demonstrated. It is difficult to determine how far these differences are related to differences in methodology, and how far they are due to differences in the conceptual frameworks and assumptions employed by researchers.

Acknowledgements:- I should like to thank Ken Mullen, Patrick West, Raymond Illsley and Audrey Hearnshaw for helpful comments and suggestions during the writing of this paper.

References

1. Walker, A. (Ed.) Rural Poverty: Poverty, Deprivation and Planning in Rural Areas. Poverty Pamphlet, 37, CPAG, London, 1978.
2. As shown by the work of the Strathclyde Regional Council Welfare Rights Team. See: Strathclyde Regional Council, Island Cost of Living: The Case for an Island Cost of Living Addition for DHSS Claimants. 1981.

3. Ritchie, J., Jacoby, A. & Bone, M. Access to Primary Health Care: An Enquiry Carried out on Behalf of the United Kingdon Health Departments. OPCS, Social Survey Division, HMSO, London, 1981.
4. Bloor, M., Horobin, G., Taylor, R. & Williams, R. Island Health Care: Access to Primary Services in the Western Isles. Scottish Consumer Council/MRC Medical Sociology Unit, 1978.
5. Royal Commission on the National Health Service. Access to Primary Care. Research Paper No. 6, HMSO, London, 1979.
6. Welsh Consumer Council. Getting Primary Care on the NHS. Cardiff, 1979.
7. Joseph, A.E. & Bantock, P.R. 'Measuring Potential Physical Accessibility to General Practitioners in Rural Areas: a Method and Case Study' Soc. Sci. and Med. 16, 1982.
8. Knox, P.L. 'The Accessibility of Primary Care to Urban Patients: a Geographical Analysis' Journal of Royal College of General Practitioners. 29, 1979.
9. Wenger, C. The Elderly in the Community: Mobility and Access to Services. Social Services in Rural Areas Research Project, Working Papers, No. 16, 1981.
10. Horobin, G., & McIntosh, J. 'Time, Risk and Routine in General Practice' Sociology of Health and Illness. 5, 3, 1983.
11. DHSS. Sharing Resources for Health in England, Report of the Resource Allocation Working Party (RAWP). HMSO, London, 1976.
12. SHHD. The Report of the Working Party on Scottish Health Authorities Revenue Equalisation (SHARE). HMSO, Edinburgh, 1977.
13. Brotherston, Sir J. Morbidity and its Relationship to Resource Allocation. Welsh Office, 1978.
14. Countryside Review Committee. Rural Communities. Topic Paper, No. 1 HMSO, London, 1977.
15. Haynes, R.M. & Bentham, C.G. 'The Effects of Accessibility on General Practitioner Consultations, Out-Patient Attendances and In-Patient Admissions in Norfolk, England' Soc. Sci. and Med. 16, 1982.
16. Tudor Hart, J. 'The Inverse Care Law' The Lancet. 1, 1971.
17. DHSS. Inequalities in Health (The Black Report). London, 1980.
18. Knox, P.L. 'Medical Deprivation, Area Deprivation and Public Policy' Soc. Sci. and Med. 13D, 1979.
19. Walker, A. 'Introduction' in Walker, A. (Ed.), Rural Poverty: Poverty Deprivation and Planning in Rural Areas. Poverty Pamphlet, 37, CPAG, London, 1978.

20. Heller, T. 'Health and Health Services' in Walker, A. (Ed.), Rural Poverty: Deprivation and Planning in Rural Areas. Poverty Pamphlet, 37, CPAG, London, 1978.
21. Leschinsky, D. Health Services in Rural Areas: A Survey of a Selected Sample of Women's Institute Members. 1977.
22. Grime, L.P. & Whitelegg, J. 'The Geography of Health Care Planning: Some Problems of Correspondence Between Local and National Policies' Comm. Med. 4, 1982.
23. Coles, O. 'Transport and Rural Deprivation' in Walker, A. (Ed.), Rural Poverty: Deprivation and Planning in Rural Areas. CPAG, London, 1978.
24. DHSS. Priorities For Health and Personal Social Services in England: a Consultative Document. HMSO, London, 1976.
25. SHHD. The Way Ahead. HMSO, Edinburgh, 1976.
26. Robinson, J. An Evaluation of Health Visiting. Council for the Education and Training Of Health Visitors, London, 1982.
27. Douglas, J.W.B. & Bloomfield, J.M. Children Under Five. George Allen and Unwin, London, 1958.
28. Butler, N.R. 'Child Health and Education in the Seventies. A Preliminary Report prepared for Members of the Association of Specialists in Community Medicine and the Society of Area Nurses' Child Health. 1978.
29. Coupland, V. & Gender, C. 'Class and Space as Accessibility Constraints for Women with Young Children' in Health Research Group, Contemporary Perspectives on Health and Health Care. Occasional Paper, No. 20, Dept. of Geography, Queen Mary College, London, 1982.
30. Horobin, G. & McIntosh, J. 'Responsibility in General Practice' in Stacey, M. et al (Eds.) Health and the Division of Labour. Croom Helm, London, New York, 1977.
31. Curtis, S.E. 'Spatial Analysis of Surgery Locations in General Practice' Soc. Sci. and Med. 16, 1982.
32. Smith, D.M. 'Geographical Perspectives on Health and Health Care' in Health Research Group, Contemporary Perspectives on Health and Health Care. Occasional Paper No. 20, Dept of Geography, Queen Mary College, University of London, 1982.
33. Eyles, J., Smith, D.M. & Woods, K.J. 'Spatial Resource Allocation and State Practice: The Case of Health Service Planning in London' Regional Studies. 16, 4, 1982.
34. Mohan, J. 'Location-Allocation Models, Social Science and Health Service Planning: an Example from North East England'

Soc. Sci. and Med. 17, 1983.

35. Hunt, A. The Elderly at Home: a Study of People Aged Sixty-Five and Over Living in the Community in England in 1975. OPCS, Social Survey Division, London, 1976.

36. Seed, P. Mental Handicap: Who Helps in Rural and Remote Communities? Costello Educational/Scottish Society for the Mentally Handicapped, Tunbridge Wells, 1980.

37. Dingwall, R. 'Health Visiting and Social Work - Where are the Boundaries?' Health and Social Services Journal. November 22nd, 1975.

38. From current research being conducted by David Hunter, Unit for the Study of the Elderly, Dept. of Community Medicine, University of Aberdeen (personal communication).

39. From current research being conducted into the attitudes of professionals in health and social work towards current policies for the care of chronically dependent people.

A PRACTICE VIEW

Stuart Watts

Is there a difference between rural and urban social work practice? Are the various different models of service delivery - genericism, specialism, casework, community work, intake teams, long term teams, and patch teams - equally appropriate to both rural and urban settings? As a rural social worker I believe that there are some differences in the social work tasks that the rural social worker is confronted with compared to that of his city counterpart and, consequently, that there are certain types of service delivery that are less appropriate for rural areas, even if they were financially acceptable to employing agencies.

The type of service delivery that is offered to the consumer, whether rural or urban, though influenced by training courses, professional associations and departmental policy, is dictated by teams of or individual fieldwork social workers and by their interpretation of what social work is all about. Is it working with individuals or families, clinically isolated from their living environment i.e. the casework/specialist/generic/reactive approach or is it working with individuals, families, groups and communities i.e. the group/community work/pro active approach? The trail of social work through the last three decades is littered with academic tomes and theories which has placed fieldwork practice, social work service delivery and consequently social workers in one of these two opposing camps. Only comparatively recently has a new method of service delivery, the generalist approach, been developing or rather being recognised, which utilises a combination of methods of intervention, from both the casework and community work camps, to approach the problems presented by an individual, group or community.

Many qualified field social workers would argue that their main function is that of a caseworker. A small minority of qualified fieldworkers are employed as community workers. The remainder would describe themselves as generic caseworkers with a specialist interest that, in a small number of cases, could be community work, and it is they who try to 'bridge the gap'; using their social work skills to work with both individuals and communities. The majority of rural social workers (especially single practitioners) are, because of the financial constraints of the department and their working situation, forced into this generalist role, whereas urban social workers may have more opportunity to choose under which social work banner they operate.

THE RURAL SOCIAL WORK SCHEME

Working as a fieldworker in a rural area can be regarded by urban social workers as an unpressurised 'soft option'. Where are the large council estates, the high rise flats, where is the deprivation in rural areas? In city/urban areas deprivation is usually visible and consequently demands a response from statutory and voluntary agencies. In rural areas deprivation often cannot be seen unless you stop your car, get out and look for it. Deprivation is often hidden behind the neat lace curtains of that quaint little country cottage, or in a tied house at the end of a farm track, down a side road in a group of local authority agricultural houses, or in a residential caravan site masked by a row of fir trees.

Deprivation exists in rural areas but it is usually isolated and remote and therefore generally overlooked by central and local government in their allocation of resources. For example, in city and urban areas there is Urban Aid, but there is no equivalent for rural areas.

In addition to the accepted measurements of deprivation such as poor housing, unemployment, over-crowding, lack of basic amenities (see Brogden), rural dwellers are deprived of a number of services that their city/urban counterparts take for granted in their everyday life, such as buses, shops, schools, Post Offices, Unemployment Benefit Offices, Social Security Offices, general medical services and even social work departments. These services may not be efficient in the city, but at least they exist. For the rural dweller they are either non-existent or a considerable distance away. In the area where I work, in the middle of Grampian Region, the D.H.S.S. is not just around the corner but 40 miles away. The Unemployment Benefit Offices is 24 miles in the opposite direction and not on a direct bus route. Specialised medical and psychiatric services are also 40 miles away and the cost is almost £6 for the return trip. Because of the infrequency of buses and trains a patient would have to allocate a whole day to obtain a half-hour appointment. The cost of basic needs i.e. food and clothing is also higher and the opportunity to 'shop around' very limited. Cashing a Giro, Pension or Child Benefit Book can be an expensive operation if, because of lack of public transport, you have to hire a taxi. This list of disadvantages is the back drop for the rural consumer and the starting point for the local social work department to consider the type of service delivery that is most appropriate for the area.

CENTRALISATION v LOCALISATION

Centralisation has to be looked at in a historical context before the advantages or disadvantages can be discussed. One has to ask who benefits from centralisation, supplier or consumer, and be aware of the fact that the centralisation of social work services has a direct effect on the type of service delivery used by the department.

Prior to Seebohm, centralisation and specialisation reigned supreme, with city/urban based offices serving large geographical areas. The type of work done by social workers was according to their specialism (child care, mental health, probation) and tended to be a reaction to a referral from other agencies. Little or no preventative work was done and access to the service was usually via a third party. After Seebohm, or, in Scotland, Kilbrandon, came genericism, which involved individual social workers dealing with all types of problems (except in England, Wales and Northern Ireland where the probation service remained a separate department).

At this time most social work departments decentralised and groups of previously specialist workers found themselves dispersed to work as generic social workers from area offices/sub-offices usually serving a defined geographical area. Access for consumers became easier, self referrals increased, and so did the opportunity to develop models of preventative social work as the workers began to identify the common problems of the area that they served. As a direct result of the growth in both size and importance of social work departments (reinforced by local government re-organisation in 1975) there developed a new breed of social worker, the social work manager.

Now social work departments are undergoing another change in service provision: the decision making power is being taken away from professional practising field social workers and given to professional administrators. This has led to a gradual movement, via the creation of intake/long-term teams, back to centralisation and specialisms particularly in city and urban areas. Social work is again losing its preventative role in the community and is reverting to its reactive role in dealing with the general public. In rural areas this return to centralisation is a slower process but there are signs from the advent of 'high tech social work' that there are financial economies in centralisation of resources and that the existence of localised rural social work offices could also be threatened.

Working in a rural area it is hard to see any major benefit which the consumer receives from the policy of centralisation apart from keeping taxes and rates down. Perhaps the only advantage centralisation has for the consumer is that it does to some extent take away personal prejudice in the allocation of local resources e.g. housing and benefits.

It is apparent that deciding whether social work provision should be centralised or localised has a direct effect on the type of social work delivery that the department can offer. Centralisation tends to suggest specialisation and therefore lack of community awareness and direct access for the consumer. Localisation suggests genericism, community work and increased access for the consumer.

CASEWORK v COMMUNITY WORK

Since the late 60's the conflict between individual casework and community work has divided the social work profession. Caseworkers have been branded as reactionary, unrealistic, mini shrinks speaking a foreign language to a client who often doesn't know the rules of the casework game. Community workers are radical, revolutionary, with a tendency to try to bite the hand that feeds them by creating problems for their employing authority. In my view social work courses are still primarily casework orientated and tend to produce social workers who expect to practise their casework skills in their chosen working environment. The expectation of most local authorities when they advertise for a social worker is that they will have casework skills. For a minority of social workers who are employed in specialist teams such as health care and child care this is valid, but for the majority of social workers who are employed in a generic capacity such skills are not the only ones required for the job. The majority of referrals such a worker is confronted with, whether rural or urban based, revolve around three main areas, finance, housing and unemployment. In most cases, these problems lie outwith the individual's control. The social worker has to consider alternative methods of overcoming such problems which may be the main cause of relationship problems within a family. This has forced many social workers into what Martinez-Brawley has termed a 'generalist approach':

> 'Generalist practice requires a worker to enable individuals, families, small groups and larger social systems to promote the best possible relationship between people and their environment'[1].

This approach, though rapidly becoming recognised as a distinct method of service delivery, can still be seen by social work professional bodies, senior officials and some social workers as a dangerous threat to professional standards. Social workers feel safer in their established casework role and for administrators of social work departments a casework approach has always appeared to be a more efficient measurement, in terms of the output or production of a department.

The interesting aspect of both generalist practice and patch systems, which could be described as a generalistic approach at a team level, is that they have been developed by individual social workers or social work teams as a response to problems encountered within the geographical areas in which they work or, as Hadley[2] describes it, as a 'bottom up process'. Hadley suggests, in relation to patch systems;

> 'It seemed that experiences of the same kind of frustration with the inadequacies of the convential model of team organisation were leading people in a wide range of different settings to come to some kind of conclusions about the changes that were needed'.
>
> 'What made this development all the more interesting was that most of the individual initiatives appeared to have been happening in isolation from each other: the wheel was being discovered simultaneously in many different parts of the social services world'[2].

Both these methods of service provision, generalism and patch systems, can be applied in either rural or urban settings as a constructive marriage between casework and community work but whereas in urban settings one could be said to have a choice between methods of intervention, the concepts of generalism and patch are often a must in servicing remote rural areas.

CASE STUDY

Perhaps the best way to illustrate the advantages and limitations of different methods of intervention available to social workers in both rural and urban areas is to take the example of a family placed in the two different environments and then to consider the appropriateness of the methods of intervention that can be offered.

> 'Mr. & Mrs A have been rehoused after living in homeless family accommodation. They have 4 children, Johnny 14, Susan 11, James 4, Sandra 2. Mr A is unemployed. Mrs A is described as depressed. Johnny has been in trouble with the police and is

on supervision, James is described as hyperactive. The family have a number of financial problems and the Social Work Department and health services consider Sandra to be an N.A.I. risk. The house is local authority, low standard and damp. There are three main reasons for social work intervention (a) The N.A.I. risk (b) Johnny's Supervision Order (c) the financial problems'.

In an urban area this family would probably live on a council estate, with the following resources available - Unemployment Benefit Office, D.H.S.S. Office, Health Centre, Housing Department, Social Work Department, Day Nursery, Play Group, I.T. Group, Community Centre plus a variety of voluntary organisations, for example, Welfare Rights Office, Mother and Toddlers Group, Tenants Association, Unemployed Group. All these resources, though not necessarily on the family's door step, can be reached by public transport.

The social work provision for this family could be undertaken in a variety of ways. If the social work department is centralised one could assume that the family have progressed through the intake team to a long-term team. If the long-term teams consisted of generic social workers, one would be allocated to the case; if of specialists more than one worker could become involved. Both these approaches would tend to be predominately casework orientated and therefore tend to concentrate on individual members and their interrelationship within the family group. One might also assume that the social worker would refer the individual client to other agencies for problems that they perceived as being outwith their social work/specialist remit i.e. benefits, housing, education, health. In this type of approach the clients would work through their presenting problems either individually or as a family group, often without using non-social work resources i.e. James and Sandra would go to local authority day nursery and Johnny the I.T. group, with little or no reference to the local resources available within the local area in which the family live.

The patch worker's approach to the same problem would be localised, generic and drawing on any specialist skills available within the team. Though still using casework where appropriate, the individual social worker would be part of a team approach which had developed a community presence and community awareness. The patch worker would therefore look at the needs presented by both the individual client and the family as a group and relate them to the resources within the patch, with a view not only to improving the functioning of the individuals and their relationships within the family, but also the relationship of the family to the social environment in which they live. This could mean that individual patch workers or the patch work team act, either independently or in conjunction with other statutory or voluntary agencies, as a catalyst in promoting new or improving existing resources within their geographical area.

In the case of Mr. & Mrs A, the patch worker, in trying to overcome their individual problems, would try to use community resources; for example Mr. A could possibly benefit from joining an Unemployed Workers' Group, Johnnny and Susan a youth club, Mrs A, a Women's Group with a creche attached, or a Mother and Toddlers Group, and both Mrs A and James could benefit from a play group. The problem with the damp and any other housing problems could be taken up by a tenants association. Not all these resources would necessarily exist within the patch, but as the same sort of problems that affect Mr. & Mrs A and family are likely to exist for other families within the area, the creation of additional resources would therefore benefit the area as a whole and be equally used by both clients and non-clients. The additional resources would also provide a wider choice for the consumer and a preventative role for the social work department.

The main difference between these two approaches is that of the public's access to social work services. If Mr. & Mrs A presented themselves at the centralised intake team, their problem might have reached crisis proportions by then. They would be seen by an intake worker who would have minimal knowledge of the environment in which the family lived or the informal network or resources that might be available there. Mr & Mrs A would therefore have become clientised, numbered and placed in the appropriate specialist package and allocated to another worker who again might not be able to identify, or have any interest in the family's living environment.

With the patch work approach, Mr. & Mrs A could still present with the same crisis, but the duty social worker would have a wider knowledge of local resources and therefore be more likely to be able to deal with the problem without necessarily clientising Mr. & Mrs A or their family. The patch work system also offers the opportunity for Mr. & Mrs A's problems to be picked up earlier through informal channels, because of the contact patch workers would have with community groups such as play groups or unemployment groups.

If one now takes the same family and places them in a rural area how practical is it to apply the same two methods of intervention? With most housing authorities, whether in an urban or rural area, re-housed homeless families tend to be allocated houses that are 'hard to let'. The 'A' family would therefore probably be allocated a house outwith the larger rural settlements. These houses built in the 1950's were used for agricultural workers and tend to be remote and isolated in groups of between 4 and 16. None of the resources available in the urban setting are available locally. In my case, the Unemployment Benefit Office is 24 miles away, D.H.S.S. 47 miles, Housing Department 30 miles, Social Work Department (sub-office) 7 miles, (Headquarters) 30 miles, Day Nursery non existent, Play Group 7 miles, I.T. Group non existent, Community Centre 7 miles, Health Centre 7 miles, no Post Office or any shops, the nearest public transport, 3 miles away, and the only transport available the school bus.

To apply the centralised model (intake teams with long-term teams of either specialist or generic workers) is conceivable, but because of the number of workers needed and the distance they would have to travel most employing authorities would find such a scheme financially unattractive. In addition the specialist or generic worker attached to the 'A' family would find that even the most basic of social work resources were not available to the family, no I.T. worker/group for John, no drop-in centre for Mrs A or day nursery for James and Sandra. Even if they did exist how would the individuals get there? The specialist case worker would also have to acquire a thorough working knowledge of welfare benefits as there is no D.H.S.S. Office immediately available to direct the family to for advice on benefit problems. For the family to telephone can also involve considerable expense and frequently an unsatisfactory explanation to any enquiry. The N.A.I. risk would also be difficult to monitor, if one takes into consideration case loads, distance and lack of other resources. It would therefore be difficult for a social worker or group of social workers to give an effective service to the family, using only casework skills. Direct access to the department would also be extremely difficult for the client.

The localised patch work approach applied in a rural situation appears to be not only financially more acceptable, but also professionally more competent. Whereas in the city you would have a generic social work team operating a patch, in a rural situation, there is more likely to be a single practitioner covering the large geographical area which, after taking into account population figures and natural community boundaries, has been defined as a patch. The rural patch worker is also faced with a lack of the most basic of resources, shops, post offices, public transport and solicitors. Though the worker may be attached to a team, contact with them may be extremely limited. The patch worker therefore cannot rely on any of the specialist skills of colleagues and is forced into a generalised role. To maximise the potential of this role it is imperative that the worker uses any support or resources that are available within the patch i.e. community workers, health visitors, doctors, play groups.

To return to Mr. & Mrs A and their family the main problem in the rural area is lack of transport. Through their own initiative they may manage to obtain regular lifts to the main centre of population but I would suggest that it is part of the social work task to consider the possibility of a community transport scheme. To overcome the shopping problem there is the possible solution of a community shop: the social worker could become involved in employment initiatives in this area. It can therefore be seen that the rural patch worker has to have a wide commitment to community development. The approach has to be on a 'major surgery' scale rather than the traditional 'band aid' image. Being involved in this type of community project and in the creation of additional resources enables the patch worker to become known in the area and allows members of the public to approach the social work department on an informal basis, increasing the preventative aspect of the social work service being offered. There is also increased access for any approach on a formal basis.

From the case study it can be seen that both types of social work approach, specialist/generic or community/generalist, in a rural or urban setting, could conceivably be used: the differences lie in the quality and depth of service received by the 'A' family and this involves two fundamental questions:

(a) How accessible are social work departments and their services to the general public?
(b) How important is the preventative aspect of social work provision?

In addition to these established forms of social work intervention there are several other types of service provision that are either being used or contemplated by various social work departments with a responsibility for rural areas.

(a) 'High Tech Social Work'

Most social work departments are in the process of considering the application of computer technology to their service and in some cases the introduction of such schemes is being used as an argument for centralisation of services.

The utilisation of advanced technology in social work e.g. computers, help call systems, could be a useful supplement to existing social work services if they are designed to allow (a) the consumer more access to the service and (b) if they allow social workers more time in their social work tasks rather than their administrative functions. In rural settings the application of advanced technology has usually led to the centralisation of that service and in my experience with the D.H.S.S., Department of Employment and recently the introduction of the Housing Benefit Scheme, the service to the individual consumer has deteriorated considerably.

The essence of social work has always been personal contact with the individual, group or community and the use of advanced technology in social work should not be allowed to change this relationship.

(b) Mobile Social Work Offices

This form of provision is currently used by some local authorities to serve both rural and urban outlying areas. The service provided tends to be information and advice giving as this appears to be what is required by the general public. Because of the lack of facilities available in such offices it would be difficult to offer any form of in depth service. One of the main problems with such a service is in choosing a site. If the unit is too conspicuous people would tend not to use it because they would be seen doing so. If the unit is inconspicuous people would not necessarily be aware of its availability. Another problem is the 'establishment of a presence' in an area. This can often take a considerable time and therefore evaluation of such a service has to be over a period of years rather than months. A mobile social work office can never totally fulfil a local authority's social work responsibility but can be used as a useful method of ascertaining the need for sub-offices to be established in different areas.

(c) Good Neighbour Schemes

This type of scheme again supplements existing social work services and has been used primarily to care for the elderly in urban situations. In rural areas such schemes might be looked at with a certain amount of suspicion: the local population would often say that they are not needed and there are already informal caring schemes. In most small settlements everybody knows everybody else, knows what they do and where they go and when they go. The local shopkeeper, postman, minister, and district nurse would also have a general overview of individuals' personal situations and be in a position to approach the social work department, but would have to know what services the department could offer e.g. home helps, meals -on-wheels. This informal system however breaks down when dealing with 'incomers' to the community who are not necessarily accepted into informal self help systems and where individuals through their own choice function in isolation to the community. For these people there must still be a direct approach to the local social work department.

(d) Barefoot Doctor

Within social work departments and ancillary services there are numerous personnel who are not qualified social workers but have regular contact with individuals and are involved in the management of their everyday living e.g. home helps, occupational therapists, sheltered housing wardens, meals-on-wheels deliverers. In addition there are many other agencies and organisations who have contact, such as health visitors, district nurses, volunteers from W.R.V.S, Red Cross, Age Concern, housing visitors, rent collectors, ministers, play group leaders, milkman, bakers and postmen. All these groups of people should at least know that a social work department exists and the services it provides and therefore when it is appropriate to advise an individual to refer himself to the social work department. Many social work departments use volunteers in a variety of roles to supplement their service but again it is necessary for the volunteer to know when to seek advice in tackling a problem. Therefore if a social work department considers using the barefoot approach there must be a minimal training for volunteers in the perception of problems and the department must offer ongoing support to individuals or groups of workers involved in the scheme.

Though these forms of service provision are often presented as 'the answer' to the problems facing social work in rural areas, they can equally effectively be used in urban situations. Within both settings all four models could usefully advertise the presence of the social work department (a) and (b) acting as formal intake teams and (c) and (d) as informal approaches. They would also, if serviced correctly, supply information and advice over wide geographical areas and consequently allow the general public to become better informed as to the variety of social work services and welfare benefits available. None of the four models can individually provide a total service to an area but are complementary to existing social work services, though they do offer a deeper 'service penetration' to the area served.

ALLOCATION OF SOCIAL WORK RESOURCES TO RURAL AND URBAN AREAS

Once again one has to look at the historical aspect of resource allocation in the area. Since local government re-organisation many rural areas previously administered by county councils have merged with urban and city areas, which used to be administered by town or city councils. In general resources spent on social work in the town/city councils were higher than those spent in the country areas, apart from a few exceptions. The reasons behind this can be explained in political terms, but can also be related to an element of mythology regarding the reality of rural life. Rural communities have always been thought to be resistant to change, intolerant of outside intervention and to have well established self-help networks. The pressures of living are assumed not to be the same as for people in the town.

It was suggested that historically low budget administrative areas (rural) would benefit through regionalisation from merging with historically high budget administrative areas and there would be a balancing of resources. In many areas, since reorganisation, the allocation of resources has been on a 'per capita' basis for what could be described as 'new social work budget headings' i.e. services to the mentally handicapped, home finding, domicillary occupational therapy, but the allocation under 'old social work budget headings' i.e. under fives, elderly and staff appears to have continued on a disproportional basis so that the balancing out of resources has not necessarily occurred. In the city/urban areas a social work department provides day nurseries for the under-fives and day centres for the elderly; in rural areas it tends to rely on voluntary effort, play groups for the under-fives and Luncheon Clubs for the elderly, organised by voluntary organisations with a minimal social work grant. The ratio between field workers and population tends to be lower in rural areas than in city/urban areas i.e. there are fewer social workers to serve a higher population because social work departments use referral rates/size of case load to govern the allocation of staff resources. No consideration is usually given to the physical size of rural areas and therefore the distance travelled by a rural field worker or that the lack of referrals could be due to the distance between the rural consumer and the social work department. City/urban areas also have additional staff resources in the form of various specialist social services, and the extra staff involved supplement the service provision supplied by existing field workers, whether they be specialist teams, generic or patch based. Rural social workers in general do not have these extra staff resources to deploy in the allocation of cases and often have to provide these services in addition to their generalist practice.

Rural areas are also disadvantaged in the allocation of supplementary social work resources. Urban Aid and Community Programme Projects are examples of the urban focus; grants to voluntary organisations also appear to be allocated with a bias towards city/urban areas. Urban Aid Grants are allocated to areas (enumeration districts) which appear on central government statistics as deprived areas with high unemployment, overcrowding, lack of amenities etc. Consequently because of the density of population in city/urban areas urban aid projects are easily identified. In rural areas the same deprivation exists but over a wider geographical area incorporating several enumeration areas; therefore it does not show on central government statistics and consequently is not eligible for any urban aid provision. The amount of urban aid received by rural areas is extremely limited compared with the large amounts used in city/urban areas.

The Community Programme Scheme is another example of a scheme designed to be implemented anywhere, but which, when put into operation, has only a limited use in rural areas. No distinction is made between the operating costs in an urban area and those in a rural area. The cost of overheads (particularily in transport) is much higher in the rural area compared to the city; this decreases the likelihood of schemes, though financially viable in an urban setting, being implemented in a rural one. It is also difficult for sponsoring agencies in rural areas to aspire to managing agency status (i.e. offering 60-100 places) with the additional financial advantages this brings to the agency.

Voluntary organisations in rural areas are also comparatively disadvantaged in the allocation of grants from central, regional or local government compared with their city/urban counterparts. Most of the larger independent charitable voluntary organisations, Shelter, Age Concern, etc., have an established city presence with a limited remit to rural areas, and these organisations because of their influence can make large inroads into any budget available to voluntary organisations within the area. In addition there are also a considerable number of other city based organisations ranging from Associations of Social Service, Citizens Advice Bureaux, Welfare Rights Centres to Red Cross and W.R.V.S. all of which often have established statutory financial support. In rural areas the number of voluntary organisations which offer a social work resource is limited and the organisations tend to be related principally to the care of the elderly i.e. W.R.V.S., Red Cross. The only new voluntary organisation that has appeared in rural communities over the past 10 years is the playgroup movement.

Setting up new agencies in rural areas to act as a resource to the social work department is very difficult particularily with regard to funding, as they tend to have the same problem (is there a need for the service?) that rural social work departments have in obtaining resources. Once the resource is available it usually unearths wide areas of unmet social work need.

CONCLUSION

In my view there are differences in social work in rural and urban areas but these lie primarily in the resources available and access to them. The constraints imposed by distance, large geographical areas, and limited resources imply for me that the generalist model may be the only feasible one for the rural social worker, whereas in urban areas it could be one of several alternative models for delivery of services.

While there are differences, social work in urban or rural settings has other similar elements and concerns. Social workers have the same range of skills available to them but it is their responsibility to relate these skills to the individual or community that they serve. No two individuals or communities are the same and therefore to say all social workers should be patch workers or specialists is inappropriate.

It is the responsibility of the social work department to match the needs of a community to the perceived role of the social worker, equating client or community satisfaction with the individual social worker's job satisfaction. The social work department's approach to service provision should serve the needs of the consumer rather than the efficiency of the department whether the service is provided in an urban or a rural situation.

Social work is working with individuals, groups or communities and using the interrelationship between them to the maximum benefit of the client by using all available resources both statutory and voluntary. Social work agencies should make the public and other agencies aware of the services that they offer and allow for easy access at a local level both formally and informally. Social work must not become detached from or unreachable to the general public, as has happened with other professional services, so that the consumers do not use the social work deparment because it is no longer responsive to their needs. It is therefore important that any decisions related to changes in service provison are endorsed by the social workers actually providing the service at field work level, since what type of service is needed is best known at this level. Social work departments should endeavour to support their field workers and encourage their innovations.

References

1. Anderson, J.D. 'Generic and Generalist Practice and the B.S.W. Curriculum' Journal of Education for Social Work. Vol. 18, No. 3, 1982, p. 39.

2. Hadley, R. 'Tapping Experience' Community Care. March 31st, 1983, p. 19.

RESEARCH HIGHLIGHTS

Second Series. Price per copy £4.50
Subscription rate for all six issues £24.00

5 Social Work with Adult Offenders (Spring 1983)

6 Working with Children (Summer 1983)

7 Collaboration or Conflict: Working with Others (Autumn 1983)

8 Evaluation (Winter 1983)

9 Social Work in Rural and Urban Areas (Spring 1984)

10 Addiction (Summer 1984)

RESEARCH HIGHLIGHTS

First Series. Price per copy £2.50

1 Decision Making in Child Care (Spring 1981) SOLD OUT

2 Normalisation (Winter 1981)

3 Developing Services for the Elderly (Spring 1982) SOLD OUT

4 Social Work Departments as Organisations (Summer 1982)